Collected Poems: a life in poetry

Heather Farmer

Copyright © 2021 Heather Farmer

ISBN: 978-0-6451873-0-4

All rights reserved. No part of this publication may be reproduced, distributed or transmitted in any form or by any means, including photocopying, recording or imaging or by any other electronic or mechanical methods, without the prior written permission of the author and publisher, except in the case of brief quotations embodied in critical reviews and certain other non-commercial uses permitted by copyright law.

Contents

Foreword 1
USA-Canada National Parks Tour 5
Dissolution 1968–1976 35
Deceit and disintegration 1964–1974 45
Four of us 1975–1978 55
Decisions 1977–1980 95
Aftermath 1978–1980 103
Sole parent 1980s 115
As he lay dying (for my friend John Wegrzyn 1977–1980) 127
Camp Creative Binna Burra 1977–1985 139
Of Dreams and Discoveries 155
A Journey along the edge of The Dreaming 1994 207
Peaceful Earth 1996 and 2021 233
The 1990s 243
Poems for the new millennium 2000–2021 255

Foreword

I recall composing this naive poem/song sixty-four years ago, aged fifteen, sitting on an ancient post-and-rail fence outside a youth hostel in the Adelaide Hills at dawn. The words fitted a well-known classical melody and I sang it over and over. I have no recollection whether I plagiarized phrases from someone else's work; I was learning poems in German by Friedrich Schiller and Johann Wolfgang von Goethe at the time:

The sun on wings of the morning rises o'er yon eastern hill
The sky with blazing beauty glows as if it's drunk its fill
Wild thoughts so pure and splendid fill my cold body until
I too could rise with the morning across the valleys could soar
And like the sun as it rises glow with its warmth too

I began writing poetry in 1948, at the age of six, probably stimulated by AA Milne's Pooh Bear and *Now We Are Six* and nursery rhymes. Those early attempts, lost long ago, elude my memory now. The poems in this collection were written during the last five decades from the 1970s to the present day. Presenting them more or less chronologically means the early, naïve poems come first. In 1960, I was an eighteen-year-old student of English Literature and Language at Sydney University, and received a scathing comment on an essay I wrote about the romantic poets: 'Naïve to the point of embarrassment'. I hope persevering readers discern growth and developing maturity in my work over the decades.

The poems were written during both challenging and exciting periods in my life. My marriage was already breaking down by 1970, but my poems start in 1975 with our first overseas trip with Tony Groom of Binna Burra Lodge and his late wife Connie. It was the inaugural USA tour for their company *interNationalParktours*. There were also national park tours to New Zealand in 1976 and Hawaii in 1981. Poems inspired by these trips found their way into *of Dreams and Discoveries*—published in 1979 and again in 1994—which tells the story of a life in poems, enhanced by Steve Parish's nature photography—and are in that section of this collection. The friendship with the Groom family began in 1974 during a family holiday at Binna Burra after which we invited them to join us in Perisher Valley on a skiing trip.

I was raised in Sydney in a loving extended family, which I describe in *The Longest Decade: a literary memoir of the 1940s* published in 2015. My parents were married for sixty years until my father's death in 1996, and I naively anticipated marrying a faithful, loyal, truthful, romantic man like my father. Engaged to Bill at eighteen, I married him aged twenty in December 1962, moved to the Blue Mountains and gave birth to three children under four before I was twenty-four. It was a conventional start—but in the sixties and seventies fidelity had become *passé* and faithfulness, loyalty and transparency were not Bill's strong points. In late 1975 we became enmeshed with another couple—we shared seven children between us—and after three years of distress, heartbreak, turmoil and near-tragedy it ended in the disintegration of both marriages and the friendship. Many of my 1970s poems reflect these painful experiences.

During this period, at the age of forty in 1977, Bill suffered a cerebral aneurism. He was critically ill, but miraculously recovered. During his hospitalisation I met another patient, a young Polish man named John Wegrzyn, who was slowly dying due to advanced neurofibromatosis. We became friends and I visited him frequently—in hospital and later in a hospice. I wrote fragments of prose about him with the title *When Johnny Comes Home* (unpublished), as well as a number of poems reflecting his experience of dying which I've included in this collection.

After Bill recovered from the aneurysm, he refused to give up his extracurricular sexual activities, so I left him—and them—to it and embarked on adventures of my own. Camp Creative at Binna Burra Lodge between 1977 and 1985 were life-changing experiences. I met many notable writers, artists, crafts-persons and musicians, including flautist Don Burrows and guitarist George Golla, artist Irene Amos, poet Peter Skrzynecki and wildlife photographer Steve Parish. During the eighties and into the early nineties I was a tour leader for *interNational Parktours*, leading groups through the national parks of the USA, including Alaska, Hawaii, Canada, the then Yugoslavia, Austria, Switzerland, Norway and England. Binna Burra was a haven during this time. I was very sad to learn that Binna Burra Lodge and Tony Groom's home were burnt down on 9 September 2019 as fires ravaged the hinterland of south-east Queensland.

The year 1977 also marked the beginning of my friendship with renowned wildlife photographer Steve Parish, culminating in two editions of *Of Dreams and Discoveries*, the first in 1979, the second in 1994. The latter edition also included the release of a DVD of the same name composed by the late Tony O'Connor.

In 1981 I moved from the Blue Mountains with my three teenage children to Grafton in northern NSW and initially lived in a farmhouse on a property at Whiteman Creek. I continued writing, including poetry, a play, novels for young adults and a number of short stories. In 1987 I met another John, who in time became my second husband. We moved to Cairns in 2001 and painlessly divorced in 2006.

The Longest Decade: a literary memoir of the 1940s was published in 2015.

Recently, in 2020, lyrics I wrote in 1996 while living in Grafton, sung by my niece Carolyn Ferrie to music composed by Bruce Vickery and Len E Johnson and published as DVDs, were uploaded online. I have included the lyrics in this collection, and the album, *Peaceful Earth*, can be accessed online on forty sites including iTunes, Apple Music, Amazon Music, YouTube Music and Spotify. Search Farmer Ferrie Johnson Vickery Peaceful Earth

I continue to write poetry, short stories and new drafts of my young adult novels with a sense of urgency. Time is running out!

Heather Farmer
2021

USA-CANADA NATIONAL PARKS TOUR

1975

The following poems were written in May–June 1975 during the inaugural tour with interNationalParktours, hiking USA and Canadian National Parks—Yosemite, Bryce, Zion, Grand Canyon, Mt Rainier, Yellowstone, Glacier Lakes, Olympic, Moraine Lake, Lake Louise, Lake O'Hara, and Glacier Bay National Monument, Alaska. Other poems written during this tour can be found in the section titled of Dreams and Discoveries.

The beginning

We
minute specks
in the dust of life
miniscule links
in the human chain
momentary thoughts
through the cosmic mind
atomic sparks of galactic flame
by some freak chance collided
when the random paths of our lives
together came

We
touching   fusing   scattering   returning
electrons   neutrons   protons
shattering   flaring   burning
using creative/creating energy
daring   learning
will never be the same

San Francisco cable cars

Humanity meets here
Lives for the moment fuse
sometimes in anger
shouting loud abuse
more often in joyous harmony
raucous laughter and yells
drowning the clanking
sound of cables—
screeching brake pads
grazing shrieking wheels
amidst the clang of bells—
while we roll with elephantine
slowness down the hills
until we reach the terminal
where bodies tumble out
in gay profusion and confusion
and a few who stand about
help the driver spin her
on the turnaround

Awe

My heart ached to find the words
to express poetically how I felt to be me
No bigger I than a leaf on a tree
or a moth in the sky

In nature's cathedrals awed by her spires
I climbed her towers contemplated her art
lay on her earth and dreamt and the rhythm
of my heart became a part of her rhythm
and I was born again into another season

I walked her timeless spaces and heard
the music that she played in every tree and stream
On turbulent seashores and tranquil bays
I watched the ebb and flow of tides and days
while moon and sun swept paths across her skies

Yosemite Falls

Water slid like liquid glass
across the track

We could not pass
and in the heat of the moment
knelt enthralled
drinking glistening gulps
in the amethyst shadows

It was then we saw them

Ranunculas
peering wistfully
through watery windows

Indian Ridge, Yosemite

'Hi!'
'G'day!'
'There's a bear up there.'
'Is there? Where?'
'Snooping around with a couple of cubs—
look out for your food! She's up to no good!'
He went on his way.

A bear up there?
Wow! How to behave!
Be cool calm and brave!
Don't feel so afraid!
We won't even see her!
She'll not show at all . . .

'There she is!' came the call

I've read about bears! Short-tempered
morose   they'll go you as quick as a flick
One slash with the claws in their paws
one crunch with the teeth in their jaws
and that's it

'For God's sake you idiot! Don't go too close!'

Hey! They're all running! I can see that bear coming
and it's not that I'm paranoid but she's looking at *ME*
and I can't climb *this* tree   it's the tallest pine in Yosemite
and *that* tree has a sign says *No Vacancy*
(which makes sense with two bear cubs in residence!)

I haven't much choice! Something's wrong with my voice
Instead of a shriek all I get is a squeak!
Shall I dive in the creek and freeze as I swim?
Or be torn limb from limb? Where's my husband? 'Bill!!!'
He's so goddam strong-willed—never listens to me!
Thinks he's so clever—just wait 'til she severs his head!

Here he comes just ahead of the bear
she on his heel!
He's sure to be killed!
Now I know how I'll feel when he's dead!

Sunset on Half Dome, Yosemite

Now that night has come
a cruel cold descends
upon the camp
the sun a vast lamp out of fuel
echoes pale gold light on Half Dome

We move around stamping boots
on granite ground damp now with dew
numb fingers thrust in armpits gloves and pockets
or held by hands warmer than our own

Silhouetted filigrees
of grey-green fir and pine
blend in monochrome
with the changing scene
on the massive granite dome

Nearby sounds the river
boiling flowing roiling foam
surging urgent icy turmoil
pounding with glancing blows
the gleaming stone
soon to fall
with soaring majesty
into the valley of Yosemite

Overnight in Las Vegas

Las Vegas—
Spanish for 'The Meadows'

There may be something in Vegas for me . . . let's see!

The croupiers are chained to their tables watched by
closed-circuit TV   A massage?   Escort service?
Ah! Amateur strip competition—now there's a possibility . . .

Or a quickie divorce—and what's more it's free!
But even in Vegas an overnight stay
is too short notice . . .

What is in Las Vegas for me?

'Shall we stay in? Or go out!'
Y'know—when in doubt
the final choice lies in a throw of the dice . . .

'In wins the toss! I'll repack the cases while you do the wash!'

(His socks are like rocks   my jeans aren't too clean
without hankies he's cranky   sweat-shirts are well-named
and if they shrink when he's washed them I can't be blamed!)

'Let's stay put! Now don't pout! Blow those neon lights out!
We can pick on these chicken bones and save on our tea
and when our work's finished you can bed down with me!'
(This bed's big enough for three or four or five
—and snake's alive there's another bed to spare!)

'Alright—don't then! Go out if you dare! See if I care!
When you deign to come back finding town rather slack
I might have some company!'

Later (much later) feeling cuddly:
'Next time we come here we could go walking.'
Silence! Is he asleep? Nah—usually he's snoring—
he can hear me alright! He's just not talking!

Well I'll be—
There's nothing and nobody in Vegas for me!

Zion

Camping out makes sense
It's the essence of simplicity
an escape from the tension and strife
profoundly present in a 'civilised' life

It's bliss to fall asleep in an open space
on a starry night with a sliver of moon

It's wondrous to wake in a natural place
feeling the warmth of the sun on your face

Like a moth in a cosy cocoon
you will emerge . . . soon . . .
knowing there's time given and to spare
to just lie quiet and be aware

Eagle Over Zion

Eagle man what's on your mind
as you scan the world with your eagle eye?

Your mind in flight goes swift and far
spiralling upward high and wide
I cannot be sure when you leave my side
that you will return to me

Eagle man what's in your heart?
The heart I hold in my hand in me?
We ignite and explode sky high
and your heart's joy is my desire
We are together and yet apart
flying wild and free

Eagle man what have you found?
What do you see as you circle round?
Your spirit unburdened by constancy
does not demand full knowledge of me
Our wing-tips touch in our life-space
where earth and sky meet face to face

Together we fly high wild and free
but I cannot be sure you'll return to me

Mountain Lion on Angel's Landing Zion

I burst into the still sunshine on Angel's Landing Zion
shattering the radiant energy which bathed that silent place

I (pink galah) hurled my raucous voice on high
stunning the slumbering air with violent vibrations
sabotaging the reflections of a quiet man sitting there

i to eye   eye to i   warily we studied each other's face
I recognized a mountain lion   coiled   shy   lithe   free
an almost extinct race of animal man

Who knows what he thought of me

Tony

I turned—my camera met his gaze in focus
I saw the radiant light playing with the shadows
on his face

For a thousandth of a second the shutter opened wide
and let him look inside where he burned a vivid impression
of his enigmatic expression and I captured his charisma
as a flame is caught ablaze

My eye the camera   the film my retina
the after-image imprinted in my mind and on this page

Mount Rainier, also known as Tahoma, is a large active volcano, with an elevation of 4,392 metres or 14,411 feet, in the Cascade Range of the Pacific Northwest, in Mount Rainier National Park in Washington state, sixty miles south-southeast of Seattle. It is surrounded by glaciers and meadows of wildflowers.

Tahoma!

Grumbling to himself
white brow frowning low
Tahoma peers with stony stare
at micro-homosapiens below

With subterranean rumbles
he clears volcanic rubble
from his glaciated throat
ridge arms folded across
the amphitheatre of his chest
Wrapped in his winter coat
he leans his razor back against
the sky andesite shoulders hunched
A remote profile   an ancient monument
with an unseen, all-seeing eye

An old volcano still alive cheeks furrowed
by ice rivers of tears wept during solitary
vigils lasting thousands of years while winds
and storms blizzards and snow
age and grind him down blow by blow . . .

It was the morning of the first day
The micro-homosapiens began their climb
with four experienced guides to lead the way

Tahoma was a feast for the eyes
Stunted firs   often on their knees before
his stormy lash   for now stood serenely
straight and green glittering with fresh snow
powder and fragile icicles

Tracing the footprints of their guides
the micro-humans   without haste
clambered up *Tahoma*'s side
and tramped across his snowy waste

'Hullo mountain! Hullo *Tahoma*!'
Hullooo mountaaain! Hullooo Tahomaaaa!
Back came the echo!
(This snow is no silent shroud
blanketing a dead heart!)
They coo-eed, yelled and laughed aloud
Tahoma took it in good part
resounding back his name

The first day's goal was reached at last
Camp Muir—two thirds up *Tahoma*'s height
the altitude 10,000 feet
In the afternoon light they stood in awe
breathing the rarefied air in gasps
Mount St Helen's, Adams and Hood
peered distantly through mist and cloud
Above them loomed the mountain's crest
draped in snow and glacial ice
Tahoma—aloof and proud—ignored
the humans on his breast

Camp Muir—stone igloos hunched
against *Tahoma*'s breath—sheltered hapless
humans from the terrors of the night
as the mountain whistled warnings
of loneliness and death
through every crack and crevice
and honeycombed waves of ice

Beneath the snow a deep rhythm was drumming
The voice in the wind was *Tahoma* humming

With the advent of the dawn the wailing
howling spirits fled and as the second day was born
the micro-humans   life-lined together
clutching ice-axes
began to ascend the face of Rainier

Crevasses!
Mere wrinkles on *Tahoma*'s furrowed face
To micro-homosapiens great yawning slashes
indigo caverns each a deep and terrifying place

Climb!   Climb!   Climb!
Breathing a hard fast rhythm
that burst out in whistling gasps
Climb!   Climb!   Climb!
The hot sweat freezing on bent back-packs
running salt into sun-cracked lips
Climb!   Climb!   Climb!
Flexing the muscles in weary hips

Don't look behind   feet follow the mind
and it's too far down   the giddy sweat
glistens in tiny beads   don't look up
the heart's courage will drown for if
watched too closely the goal recedes
The sky comes down to meet the snow
and it doesn't *seem* very far to go . . .
but it isn't easy to touch the sky
even if only with the eye

At last!
Clambering over *Tahoma*'s brow
they stumble onto his andesite head
resting bodies that tremble now
on the snow and ice and grit of his bed
They laugh and hug and kiss each other
photograph the summit and one another
gasping and shouting their triumph and praise
for the glorious gift of these past two days

Olympic NP Washington State

She is loved again

Her jewelled leaves shine
with a translucent sheen
a tender young vine
transparently green
loved by the rain

The spider's song

Radiant glow
of sunlight through silk

The spider's song
a silent symphony

Light and song
caught in a web
of music

An Alaskan fairy tale
Glacier Bay National Monument

Once upon a time in Alaska I was left behind—
or rather I preferred to stay than face a glacier climb
or walk a long way to nowhere in particular
Instead I wandered along the shore of Glacier Bay
feeling strange to be alone in this bewitched
bewitching landscape

Behind me the enchanted forest beckoned
Shafts of dancing light emerald green—the like
of which I'd never seen before—flickered
on the forest's mossy floor which merged
with the juniper along the beach's pebbly shore

The reluctant sun gradually relinquished its fragile grip
on the darkening sky its fading light glowing
like shattered amber on the wind-indented water
I knew for sure with apprehensive certainty that
at this magic moment separating night from day
middle-earth held sway

The memory of this place still—even now—fills me
with haunted wonder for here where I had caught a glimpse
of movement in the forest like light on rippling water
I came face to face with Earth's daughter!
She came out of the green light dancing laughing leaping
full of feeling overflowing with the joy of living

Then I saw another!
In flight he came like the spirit of Pan!
They were wanton and free as they could be
living loving and giving   living to love   loving to live
loving and living flowing together the one co-existing
with the other not for the taking but for the giving

I did not see them going but felt their energy
flowing as I staggered reeling down onto the beach
beyond their reach quivering with the knowing

Even now
though time has passed so that it seems long after
I shiver to remember . . .

Iceberg
Glacier Bay National Monument, Alaska

Inchoate snow seed in a glacial womb
gestated for eons of time until—
bearing down the maternal valley
—you were calved full grown
forcibly pushed with slow finality
into the sea to take your place
as refuge for the herds of seals
and countless seabirds in Glacier Bay

One stormy day you floated
dangerously close to shore
Urged by the wind
the waves bore you in their arms
and threw you way beyond their reach
onto this beach where you now lie
a frozen wreck   a massive monolith
an icy mountain doomed to die
slowly dripping your life away

The iceberg and the stone
Glacier Bay National Monument, Alaska

The iceberg embraces a granite stone

A strange relationship
he forced to hold and nurse her
though her warmth
absorbed from the sun
is melting him away
day by day

They came from different worlds
she from earth forged in fire
he from air birthed from water

For eons he carried her
through tunnels of darkness
until   eventually   locked together
the iceberg calved from the glacier
and fell into the sea
where they floated and drifted
sunlight gradually turning
his indigo heart to white
until a storm and tidal surge
left them stranded on this beach

Now day after day after day
and night after night
unaware of his plight
the warmth of her gaze
is imperceptibly
melting him away

Airport

Here where rendezvous began
the first becomes the last
scene of the play
as private dreams
played out in public drama
suffer their final *denouement*

No great tragedy
The protagonists
merely have to say goodbye

It's just that in this final act
the magnetic forces
of cohesion and fusion
once so compelling
have lost their charge
as currents   turning awry
repel the players against their will
negative from negative away
to wander back to separate lives
somewhat aimlessly

South Island, New Zealand
Milford Sound to Lake Te Anau
(for Jules 'Tiger' Tapper)
1976

Meet a bushman bearded lean and hardened
to a life where deer are killed for profit
and planes and choppers boats and feet
are transport in terrain that's difficult
and there's no other way

They call him 'Tiger' Tapper and sometimes
he flies tourists over Martin's Bay
up into the skies above the mossy forests of beech
into the crags and outcrops on the mountain tops
where even goats can't climb!
What an experience!
A once-in-a-lifetime if you're a tourist
Jules does it every day and he's learnt to cut it fine

If you want to discover how it feels
to be an eagle soaring on a wind current
up and over the saddle between the peaks
dropping suddenly weightless down a glacier
then swooping up in a flowing curve
and banking in a sweeping arc
that sends your heart into your leaden feet
shrieking through the Sound the shadow
of your outstretched wings streaking
along the canyon wall . . . while Jules fills out
his logbook seemingly not watching
where he's going at all . . .

If you want to see the grandeur
of these mountains not yet climbed
and the vast design of nature stretching
out before you like a map in unknown hands . . .

If you have no fear of dying and like to be excited
by the feeling of being high
reeling and wheeling through the sky
while the whole world falls away below . . .
let Jules 'Tiger' Tapper take you flying!

DISSOLUTION
1968–1976

1

Beloved
I have often talked with you
I cannot tell you what we've said
for I have always listened
with my heart and not my head
I have tried to get the meaning
rather than the words
but now I'd like to tell you
what I feel it was I heard

Love is essentially seeing
what I can do for you
Love is essentially being
what you need me to be
Love has no expectations like:
'What can you do for me?'
or subtle manipulations
implying responsibility
for what has happened
or 'Look what you've done to me!'

Love is essentially freeing—
I know that the way I feel
is because I am what I am
My emotions are not caused by you
they come from inside *me*
because of how *I* feel and think
and how *I* want to be

Love reaches beyond emotional refuse
transcending hostility and debate
and manipulation and ventilation
of insecurities needs and hate
Love is trusting and lays no blame
It's commitment and sharing
collaboration co-operation
and truly caring

But it means holding on to each other
making sure that nobody cries
It requires being loyal to each other
to be loving in each other's eyes

2

Indifference is uneasy
hiding in the hollow
question-mark
around tomorrow

Lines are drawn like blinds
against the now
on the perpetual calendar
of a life circled with reminders
of commitments
remembering only
yesterday's imprisonment

3

Compelled by duty not by pleasure
they rise with the sun
live and move with the seasons

No voluntary impulse awed by the elemental
inspires his fidelity or her desire

In bondage to cold hard reason
more real than the games people play
in harmony with life's perpetual cycle

constrained by contracts conditions penalties
his debt to her remains intact security attached

The favours she has done he cannot repay
Owing to each other with no release
from the debtors' prison to this end they have come

4

Beyond the curling veil
of careless words   silence
barren as the wilderness of pity

Unenlightened expressions of thought
lost in the darkness of anxiety
unable to hear or see

. . . why prolong the living of the corpse?

but only touch and feel
the shape of torn ideals
once warm   intense
now withered dreams
unknown forms without identity

Voices crying out
in the realm of the mind
on planes of detachment
for release from the prison
of desire to make sense

5

Small nibbles of bland

Smooth colourless words
tepid as blood

Between the knife and the fork
small-talk

The weather perhaps?

Perhaps it will rain?
Perhaps it will flood!

Perhaps clouds will shift
and the sun will shine?

Perhaps   pass the salt

(I don't give a damn!)

Babes-in-the-woods
Eat your paps

6

This man is tender
that one's tough
This man is gentle
the other one's rough
This man is fair
the other's unjust
This man is truthful
the other don't trust
This man is honest
the other tells lies
This man loves me
the other wrecks lives

This man will always be a friend
The other will be lonely
in the end

DECEIT AND DISINTEGRATION
1964–1974

1

You litter
her crumpled bed

The crumbs
of your dried-up tears
discomfort me

It's over   done   finished with
my heart an empty gourd
now filled with round flat lies
and I must drop each one
into the space behind her eyes

Go back to anonymous streets
where time and false perspective
will direct you to a point
outside my mind

Don't try to climb my wall

She must not know
that you were here

You were not here
at all

2

Okay! Okay! Okay!

So he's done the dirty on me!
Not to worry—my turn will come one day

The bum!
Screwing other women
all these years of unheeded tears
while I shrivelled up in my marriage
prison and wasted my life
being a faithful wife

I've got to admit
he played the game in fine style
the hypocrite—telling me lies
with sickening innocence
without a flaw
full of loving words
meaning none of it

He's shit!
Not worth the spit
that sticks in my craw
What a waste of *my life*!
Why didn't I trust my sixth sense?
Instead
while he's philandering
in other beds
I—suspicious—overwrought
thought what a witch I was
a neurotic bitch
a jealous housewife
with not enough to do!

To think I thought he could not tell a lie!
What a sucker!
To think I had such faith in the stinking guy!
What a fucker!
But not to worry—it's okay okay okay by li'l ol' me
One day my day will come too
and it will be stiff shit   tough luck   thumbs up
get fucked my love
to you!

3

Ephemeron

Spirit biding inside inner tensions
Free mind wheeling   inconstant nebulae
spiralling to depths of cool dimensions
down into the shadows of uncertainty

Love is a spectrum of colours
diffused through dim participation
Not knowing   like lying
is not growing   but growing confused
not going beyond what love perceives
as thin ice dangerously

The spring of love overflows
—joy felt with crystal clarity
Beneath   within   by desire drowned
a lost reflection of tears cried
when fusion becomes confusion
and separation

4

What am I to you?

No more than a seed in your apple
and you've thrown away the core
having sucked my juices
and eaten the rest of me
skin and all

Though you'll forget me when I'm gone
the rain will weep   the sun will shine
and I will grow and blossom again

You've taken everything
I had to give except my life

And I will live

5

From my capsule
I can see it all
like a map of *us*
every way I look
surrounding me
And yet I speed away
a shrinking nucleus
a compacted mass

We will divide
like cells
He'll take a part
of me with him
I'll take a part
of him with me

Memories
are empty shells

All he has
is the shell of me

6

Everybody!
Watch me go!

Race I down bright arc of sunshine
swiftly sail white bowl of snow
a cornflake in a sea of milk
sliding through the knife-edged
shadow into folds of corniced silk

You'll never know how much
I want to play within this life of mine
Take me wind and leave no sign

I now know nothing of grief or guilt
Upon my many-sided face
pure white there is no trace

You cannot stop me
let me go
a snowflake in a fall of snow

Four of us
1975–1978

Wednesday, the twelfth of May 1976
(For Vaughn Croser, aged 11, who died after a battle with leukaemia)

Vaughn?
Sometime sunshine friend
I thought I heard an echo
of your laughter
through the crack of dawn
An early bird maybe
but I followed the sound
into a quiet moment
where I found you

I did not know
today would be the day
you'd decide to go
You died before you
finished saying
what you were
trying to explain
on Sunday

You knew then—didn't you?

I watched your face when
you spoke about going away
to another place—
about feeling no pain—
how everything was 'silvery'

Was it like a speeding train
where you open the door
reach across a windy space
and open the other door?
Caught halfway
between here and there?
Between yes and no?
Unsure whether to stay or go?

You were frightened then
feeling alone not quite ready
to leave your home but today
Wednesday the twelfth of May
Who helped you decide to go?

1

Trees can speak

I'm pleading with you to let me reach
with words across the silent space
we keep between us

I'm needing to touch you now
share your mind somehow
feel how you feel and whether you care
discover what is and what is not real between us

It's too easy to talk without speaking—
to speak without saying
what's really on my mind
Silence has its reasons

I can control my actions—but deep
inside me stirs a loving caring spirit
and the quelling of it is more difficult

This need to communicate on a real level
lies like a dormant seed waiting to be born
while we wait out the seasons with our eyes
speaking without words

This seed of friendship
can grow like an enduring tree
as long as it is not damaged or broken
or bruised or shaken
Perhaps that which I long to know
should never be spoken

Will I ever know?
I listen and hear the trees
sighing in the forest shadows
I listen to the leaves whispering
patterns on the sky or murmuring
on the forest floor before they die

Perhaps we hear each other talking like the leaves
Perhaps I already know without actions or words

2

Want to know
how much I care?
Hold me near

Feel the flow
of the love we share
as we lie here

If you can't tell
if I'm for real
just watch my eyes

You'll know full well
what I really feel
they can't tell lies

You are a man
and for you I keep
a secret part of me

I am a woman
our love is deep
May it always be

3

Lying together in the bed
still and softly sleeping
toe to toe   head to head
in each other's keeping

Desire ebbs and flows
on currents of emotion
bodies drawing close
adrift upon love's ocean

Floating side by side
breath like crosswinds blowing
lifting softly on a tide
of mindless feeling growing

Dreams in free-flight wheeling
in the darkness there
Thoughts on wings of feeling
cleave the dreaming air

They stir and move together
at their ethereal caress
and turn towards each other
to share their happiness

She sleepily unfolds
at his touch upon her skin
He whispers as she holds
him: *I love you let me in*

Thoughts and dreams merge
and sink in the surging sea
The lovers—now submerged
—drown in ecstasy

4

Brown alive beautiful alive brown
Dark is night is dark
Feel me please please feel me

The grass is wet is the grass
o beautiful sounds beautiful o

Higher higher go we go higher higher
O my god together my love

Hold me

JR

5

Please don't hold me back from flying!
How much time have I left to try
before you leave me with my crying
when our season of love begins to die?

There's not one night there's not one day
I spend with you that's thrown away
or burned or used up without reason
How many days left in our season?

***6**pyt*

Reunion
17/04/1976

    While I was away I said
    to myself I said (feeling sad)
    It's not just a matter
    of going to bed
    Much more important
    is loving the friend
    Friendship began it
    and if love should end
    may the friendship remain
    But (o my god)
    my beautiful friend
    I am glad to be
    in your arms again!

7

Who am I?
Who are you?

You laugh and cry and yawn and sigh
and sleep the same as I do
You gaze at me intently or wander
with your eyes outside
keeping your thoughts inside
your feelings undercover
and I can touch and stroke your skin
but cannot truly enter
cannot quite come in

I am outside
You are inside
We are separate though together

My life unravels in another place
from yours—you live in a different space
The smile that comes to your face
when we look at the same thing
leaves me sombre

We are different you and I
Us and *we* do not mean
we are joined together
merged as one
never to ever come undone

We are apart
Though I hold your hand/take you in
share my body/my life
my feelings/my thoughts/my mind
we are not one
One of us is always in front/beside
behind or left behind
But still I want to be with you
feel your warmth/your strength
enclosed in your arms I am almost inside
by your side sleeping wrapped around you
I am almost almost inside inside
but not-quite never-ever quite inside your skin

8

Last night I dreamt . . .

I saw you climbing
boxes   rocks   a shelf
reaching out for an open bottle
above your head

until you fell with a yell
and all the boxes   rocks
came tumbling down

But someone saved you
just before you smashed
your head on the concrete floor
stoned dead

They put you in a shoebox
with the lid across your face
which I removed
so you could breathe
but they pushed me aside

'Leave him alone!' they said

They took you out
painted your face
stuck on moustache and beard

And then you began
to dance and spring about

Doubtful I came closer
and saw the puppet strings

My dreams are weird!

9

I want to scream!
There is no time for *us*!

I fight to see you
crammed into a space of time
not enough
the endings too abrupt
caught in the grind of things to do
too much   I miss you
to see   talk to   and touch
but it's never the right moment
to interrupt!

Can we walk again *soon*
by running water clear as glass?
Take time to picnic laugh and talk?
Make love again before we sleep
entwined upon the grass?

We are sad-faced puppets pulled by strings
facing death beneath a silver moon
manipulated raggy-saggy things
dancing to life's tune

There is no time

This is no dream

10

Being

unseen
unseeing
turning
touching
hesitating needlessly

clutching
clinging
holding
hurting
suffocating painfully

loving
hating
finding
losing
fighting desperately

slipping
sliding
calling
falling
sinking endlessly

slowing
stretching
finding
feeling
surfacing gradually

11

Do you feel humble or had?

Glad for the expression and chance
but left with the impression
you're being led in a dance
where the steps are laid out
and so are you?

Take care not to be untrusting
of the untrustworthy cad!

12

It's good to have a diversion—
especially a meaningful one
It irons out the crinkles
in the marriage-bed
She's important—but not essential
if I had to make a choice
(I don't like to say that
but it has to be said)
When all's said and done
she's a loving caring woman
She gives me a chance
to practise tenderness occasionally
and there's unlimited potential
for having fun

I don't regard it as perversion—
she's the marzipan icing on my cake
I can have it and eat it too!
Making love to her is quite exciting
Sometimes I want her very *very* much
She has a calming effect on my psyche
Distress is when I ring and can't get through

But also comes a time for switching off
One can't   I find   allow oneself
to become totally immersed
I mean that's a sure way to drown!
I have to separate the good times with her
from the rest of my strife
So when it's time to get dressed
she goes west—right out of my mind

I can't have needs! All needs must stop!
An hour ago I decided to go in an hour

which means I have to go right now!
I can't hang on five minutes or so—
I should have gone five minutes ago!

I shut off that life and return to my wife
'Are you okay?'
'Okay about what?'
'Are *we* okay?'
'No we are not!'

Distress is she no longer wants *me*
(she prefers my lover's husband so much more!)
Distress is she dislikes me very much
She weeps for *him* behind her slammed shut door
while I bash on it with turds of words
and smash her prized possessions on the floor
in a destructive and dangerous fit of jealousy
'Why can't you be like me? Is that really such a difficulty?'

Christ! To think my other woman is distressed
because sometimes can't be all the time!
I guarantee she wouldn't be so keen to be mine
if she could see me in this goddamned fucked-up mess!

13

'Leave me some stairs to climb . . .'
One of the very first things I said

So what does she do?
Drags me up two fucking stairs at a time
'til I'm half dead!

Where do we go from here?
she demands to know
from the top of nowhere
Jesus woman!
Is that all you've got to say?
What made me follow you?
It's a helluva long way down!
A man's gotta be insane—
a goddamned fool

It's dark and cold and windy
Any minute it's going to rain
Down there are the city lights—
other people warm and enclosed
while she whines and cries:
I hate heights! I feel so exposed!

I'll leave her up here on her own
turn around   hang on tight
close my eyes
and
climb
back
down
again
alone

14

He
blind to her
so many years
is blind to me now
wanting her alone
and weeping bitter tears
because once lost
she now has found
her own way home

15

Love eats into me
eroding my resolve
to be an independent woman

My life cannot revolve
around his needs
He is only a man!
Why love him desperately?
Why try to belong
or become a part of his life
when I've just won my freedom?

He thinks he has the right
to possess me
How wrong he is!
Whatever course I take
or decision I make
will come from the precision
of my own mind

16

Ignorance is cruel
His lack of awareness
or perception
of my needs
eats into my soul

He suffers too
not knowing what to do
refusing to acknowledge
that mutual love
requires that he
contribute something too

Indifference shields me now
from distrust and doubt
disappointment replacing jealousy

You go numb after a while
Chronic pain in the same place
exhausts the brain's receptors

Now I can only wonder why
I shared my space   this place
and gave away my peace
piece by piece by piece

17

I can't be bothered anymore!
What is the use of trying to explain
the same thing over and over again?

He'll never see my point of view

It's very simple   he doesn't want to

He will dismiss my every word:
'You are over-emotional   hysterical   absurd!'
He gives little but expects much

He says he feels close to me
Such an illusion!

The fact is we are far apart

Why   when I see it all so clearly
does confusion eat my heart?

18

Beware my girl!
You're about to lose
the ethereal care
you've tried to throw away

It's up to you to choose
on this last hurl
whether you want it to
come back and stay
or never return to you

19

Cold toes
Hot mouth
Sharp tongue
Facing south
Back to the sun
Joyless miserable
lack of fun
Only emotion
when she is angry
Tight with tension
Barely living
Rarely lovely
or sorry or giving
or open or trusting
or feeling compassion
Afraid to express her needs
or her passion

She hates me!
Why worry?

Because she *is* me!

20

Now is the winter of our discontent . . .

You tear her ragged
but she will not cry

She turns cold-shouldered
From your cruel oppression

You can't suck her in
with your monosyllabic staccato

She knows   once she's beaten
you'll spit in her eye

She'll die first   freeze-dried
rather than hug your cold front

You can taint green with grey
Wipe her out with white streaks

Blow her away
Bury her in drifts of depression

Exposed by shifts in her mind
is an indelible impression of summer

21

She can never be a substitute for me
for we   in our own ways   are irreplaceable

I am I   and she is she
and the roles we play and the spaces we fill
can never be interchangeable

Nor would I want to take her place

Together we make the heart and the soul

Apart we break and destroy the whole

22

Well-honed crazy bitch!
You've done it now!
Bared your bones you witch
And come undone
Hashed it well and truly

All those well-kept secrets
like a dose of shit
tumbled out somehow
Jealousies   fears   insecurities
No tears will wash away
a single word of it

There's no way he'll forget
no more will you
the things that each one said
lying in bed in the dark

Words in the night
seem to be more true
than those said in the day

Not blessed with light
or light with jest
they come out stark
shadows of thoughts
best left unsaid
locked inside the heart or head

There's no way to renew
the trust I used to feel
No way to erase the damage done
I said his love was not enough
Love that is real has no
such limitations as those
he's placed on me

Yet could I be mistaken?
Am I a fool to feel unloved
because he's not fulfilled
my expectations?

23

He's not part of my rhyme
I have nothing to say
I won't ask him to give me
so much as a line
I'll write my own way

His love is not mine
but my heart is my own
I never belonged
in his life or his home

I won't try again
to follow his mind
on this line of part-time
I'll have my own say

I'll soon find my place
in this space within space
to sing me my song
from inside my poem

When I go away
I don't yet know when
some day or one day
what will I do then?

It will come time to go
tomorrow or soon
I'll be somewhere but nowhere
where he'll hear my tune

24

God it's hard being a mother!
I've tried to give to each
their share of attention

I gave birth in all innocence
Spent my time dreaming
about the lovely times we'd spend together

It was all nonsense!
Instead I hear myself screech:
'Leave me alone!' at the end of my tether

They're so jealous of one another!
Trying to fairly reach each one
creates such tension

I've only got to mention
I need some time to myself
and they start bitching

The air is full of dissention
They constantly quarrel and fight
while I sit twitching

Why can't they be nice to each other?
I try to fill the breach
but I am so unhappy I am out of reach

Why can't I retire and go on a mother's pension?

25

I have it on good advice
know nothing
shed no tears
confide no fears
and eke out your love
like dust across the years

Drown all yearnings
to possess the lover
who whispers of lust
for another on your breast

Remember there is nothing
nothing for a lover
nothing to hold
but temptation to imagine
there is truth in the lies
that are told

And have no name!
When lovers are asleep
they are all the same

Never feel hunger
as you starve to death
for already everything's eaten

Open your eyes
and see yesterday's dreams
swallowed by tomorrow's emptiness

Accept the beautiful lie as the truth no less
though you lie in terror in a cold sweat
cowering with desire and guilt
against the love beneath the quilt

There is one last thing you must never forget:
The more you demand the less you get
If you really want your love to live
Don't expect to receive . . . just give and give

26

My sons—
what can I say?

Learn to love—
or be undone one day

Make not of love
a contest to be won
nor put it or your lover
to the test

Do not have more than one
love at a time
for eventually you will
have to choose
and then could lose
the one you chose as best

Who loves me less?
The man I married
who visits his mistress
in spite of my distress?
Or the other
also with wife and children
who visits me regardless?

They are the tides of my life
One threw me here
where I now lie
a cold stone out of reach
and I could die
waiting forever
for the other to sweep me
from this beach

Love is like the sea
both wide and deep
but lovers drown
when torn from the arms
of the other in their keep

27

I borrowed you
one yesterday
and like a child
thought I could play
you straight away

I was mistaken

I was rapt
and without guile
I did not know
your tuning changed
from day to day

My childish song
seemed harsh and strange
the timing wrong
Your strings were taut
and out of tune
the tension changed
No music could be wrought
from them at all

One by one your strings all snapped
communication broken
And when I could no longer play
I gave up trying and went away
and left you there forsaken

28

Driving into the sun
late in the day
I startled him on a curve
He rose from shadows
cast by harsh grey gums
slid with sickening hurt
across the windscreen
and plummeted to earth

I braked in a cloud of dust
and backed to where he lay
talons clenched   beak open
golden wings outspread
I struggled from the car
cradled him in my arms
stood with him on the edge
where steep slopes
in golden sweeps
rolled down to patchwork farms

Contemplating his being
my tearful eyes unseeing
I felt a presence leave him
where the beat of his heart had been
while a golden bird   another
skimmed the golden grass
in the golden heat
brushing my face with her shadow
as she passed
calling   again and again
for him to follow

I stood there with the empty bird
and felt my own heart's beat
I heard the cry of the other
hollow in the evening sky
beyond my reach
and I cried too
tied to the earth by a dead bird
and leaden feet

DECISIONS
1977–1980

1

A lone leaf
clings to a wintry morning
afraid to leave the bough
caught between loneliness and the fear of falling

Such is the now

A time to choose
between two avenues

And the wind is calling

2

Last night was the longest night
Today is the coldest day

And I am leaving you
running away

You are unforgiven

There is no way back

Signposts have been torn
from the earth

My heart—like the door
that I once opened
every time it was approached
by you—has closed

Now I do not know
not only where I live
or where I'm going
but how long it will be
before being lost
becomes another journey

3

A tactic in war is strategic withdrawal
(another name for defeat—
in that particular action at least)

I am outnumbered by forces
with which I cannot compete
I cannot change sides
or compromise my values or beliefs

They imprisoned and tortured me
(speaking metaphorically)
I was brainwashed and tricked
to suit their politics

Strategic withdrawal—not headlong flight
—a planned escape starting with my mind

My children?
The question is fraught!
So many are lost in war
What is better for them?
To be caught in the crossfire
or have one parent?
Father or mother—does it matter?
It will have to be one or the other

I have dis-illusioned me and faced reality

Beyond this marriage prison
is a line of trees—the backwoods of my mind
There I will hide and bide my time
keep my sanity and survive
until my getaway

4

Aching to escape
to an unknown place
straining   poised
on the edge of nowhere

No one holds the leash
No one is here but my self
and my reflections
Dried-up faces
upside-down moons
in the stainless sterility
of detergent washed spoons

I'll find this place tomorrow
though I don't know where

I want to go but don't yet know
how I'm supposed to get there

5

Jerked
into frightened wakefulness
by constant dreaming

images elude
my rude awakening

Simplify
connecting lines of thought
choose which path to take
cut all ties which threaten

It is essential to forget

6

The light is extinguished

Moon and stars
descend in silence
with the dark

They were my friends

Our conversations
have ended

Aftermath
1978–1980

1

Tasmania 1980
Cradle Mountain: Lake St Clair NP

Distance has no end   only approaches

Footsteps lay their tracks in mud
the waiting day grows longer
and my life is left behind

Silence crowds my solitude

No grasses whisper   clouds are hushed
ants climb noiselessly in shadow

I will disappear on my own track
leaving my voice in air   my boot-prints there

They will find my pack next summer
shrouded in mildew

No sign
to say which way
I've gone

2

Tasmania 1980
Cradle Mountain: Lake St Clair NP
Cephissus

Time distances words
space separates
until they cannot speak
of what they shared
in a dark place
close together
the mirror of the night
reflecting their blank faces

Time hung suspended

Daybreak avoided
a tangible mask to hide
behind
senses imprisoned
perceptions hidden
no questions asked
no answers given

Anonymous again
they ploughed through
black mud and white rain
Tasmanian summer ended

3

The sea beats upon the shore
washing with waves
the grey unyielding stones
shifting pebbles beneath my feet
wearing away the skin
around my bones
while I
a silent shadow
watch the tide reach
out towards the moon
bleached and hollow
above the lonely beach

4

You feel cold clear water
Your bright eye is the white sun
in a shy sky

Alive is fun
I am free to be full of laughter

The wind and I meet like rebels
rippling the water
brown cold feet
on round gold pebbles

Here I can be—
the wind in my hair
the sun on my face
—free to be me!

5

Rain
curls the ashes
of quenched desire

It came
with the tormented wind
too late to change the mind that's gone

Contorted with demented art
black slashes cut the backdrop sky

Perceptions of reality
distorted by the rape
of fire

6

Lyrebird

Hiss and crackle of burn-off
Voices on the two-way
Distant radio-hum
A chainsaw roars and stalls
Echo and rattle of rockfalls
More earth gives way
gathering momentum

Interspersed through it all
countless bird calls

She listens enthralled
in the gathering dusk
of an autumn day

until he senses her presence
catches her eye
and shyly fades away

Fire   rockfall
haunting mimicry
and birdsong
gone

7

Watch the devi
of the sky
motionless
on living wings
hanging
from the rising sun
on her last flight

A deadly shadow
sights his gun

The crack startles

With sickening hurt
she hurtles to earth

Bird and morning broken

The sun and her beak drip blood
an accusation unspoken

8

Chellonia depressa

Buried like ancient history
she woke and heard
the music of the sea

Linked by instinct
to her ancestors
who hauled their hulks
by night onto this shore
in answer to their own
primeval call
she gathered all her strength
and struggled free

Heeding the primal urge
to reach the water
oblivious to marauding hordes
swooping down and scooping up
the others marked for slaughter
she made her perilous run
towards the surf and the rising sun

Slipping into the vast eternal ocean
cradled in its surging perpetual motion
the tiny turtle in the sunlit deep
swam unerringly towards the reef

9

It's only sea-spray rolling down my back
sand sifting softly through my toes
wind whispering a smell of sea
taste of salt recipe

Sky faded blue hangs low
with slate-grey cloud
and a foghorn's echo
on a green-sea horizon

Seagulls and children call aloud
almost to each other for a share
of scraps of attention

The bitch on heat roams up and down
the beach restless suitors yelping
begging for relief

Do they feel their senses fed
pleasured by the jewelled spumes
of sculptured foam through which
they delicately tread?

Blue bottles quiver like flotsam
pulsing with silent life
in the gleaming foam along
water-washed scalloped edges
alive with refracted light
where the tide has been

I sit in harmony with my friend
enclosed in an aura of thought
in harmony with the day's soft end

10

Mourning sandpiper

You linger on the shore of her soul
living driftwood without a goal
head on a pillow of plumage
waiting for her

Lonely as a lute
your song stirs empty air

Sad as a flute the notes come
one by one calling her

How long will you love like this?
Keeping tryst?

The tides and time
will wash away all trace

No footprints there
No piping in the air

Nothing to mark the place

SOLE PARENT
1980s

1

You couldn't call it a still night
the air burping and chirping
as if frogs and crickets
came down with the rain

Black quilt draped over the sky
down there   me upside down
the moon below swimming
with stars out of sight

Cow calls her calf
The pump turns on and off
The fridge eats electricity
with a delicate grinding
yum yum hum

Yet the night itself is silent

2

I am alone

Small circle of warmth and light
keeping out the cold and dark

Sounds of fridge
dripping tap and water pump
throbbing echoes of my heart

Struggling moths
on their nuptial flight
break the silence of the night
fluttering on the windowpane

My children sleep   breathing   stirring
I share their dreams know their minds again

Again

They chose to come with me
when I moved here to another nest

Now   bereft   you are alone
cold and depressed in the emptiness
you share with the pain I left

3

I have lost my Muse!
I cannot write a word
It's all been said before
heard and done before
I'll slip over the edge of night
into the canopy of the forest
and hug a living tree!

No words needed
I'll just listen to the creaking
stretch of branches overhead
and lean and feel it settle
holding firm against the pressure
of my body rooted in its bed

And I'll stroke the warm coarse bark
If I pull away loose strips
I'll feel the smoothness underneath
Just to smell the sap rising
and hear the rhythm of its heart
will be enough for me

4

New poems spin
aimlessly
down blank pages
of sky
falling like leaves
onto the surface
of my mind

where they
float away
into the haze
illuminated by
scribbled tracks
of enlightenment
watched by
my mind's eye

Afraid of losing
a phrase or line
I unconsciously
hold my breath
lest the wind
sinks the words
to a death
not of their choosing

5

Teenage Rock

So much noise!

I am not a part of it

I fall apart because of it

It makes no sense

They are immersed
protected by it
as silence protected me

Now I have no defence

My meditations are shattered
by wavelengths lapping my feet

Soon I will drown like the silence
engulfed in hopeless defeat

The heroic exploits of Elizabeth Batts Cook, wife of Captain James Cook

She let him go though it broke her heart
allowed the farewells with the setting of the sails
Three times she watched him embark and depart
Explorer   Navigator   Cartographer
Captain of HM *Bark Endeavour*

There was freedom in living separate lives
each setting their own course—able to do
whatever they chose within the limits of their roles
the times and their places within it—
except she was left to give birth on her own
nurse three dying babies scarcely grown
mourn her children's untimely deaths alone
She was a woman of equally heroic spirit

Three times she bravely watched him depart
hoping he would return safely
The third time he did not . . .

Note:
Cook's first commission was in 1766 as Commander of HM *Bark Endeavour* for the first of three Pacific voyages taken over an eleven year period—
First Voyage 1768–1771, Second 1772–1775, Third 1776–1779

Elizabeth Batts Cook, born 4 February 1742, died 13 May 1835 aged ninety-three. She married James Cook on 21 December 1762, she not quite twenty-one, he thirty-four years old.

Married for seventeen years, they were 'together' for only four of those years. She bore him six children—five sons and a daughter—and, like her husband, they all died before her. She was a widow for more than fifty years.

James Cook was born 27 October 1728 and died 14 February 1779 aged fifty, stabbed and drowned in Kealakekua Bay, Hawaii.

Their children:
James born 1763—died 22 August 1794 aged thirty-one at sea
Nathaniel born 1764—died 1780 aged sixteen at sea in a hurricane
Elizabeth born 1767—died 1771 aged four
Joseph born 1768—died 1768
George born 1772—died 1772
Hugh born 1776—died 1793 aged seventeen of scarlet fever

For John on the birth of his grandson Joel
(born Tuesday 17 October 1989)

A child was born
child of your child
not mine
while I waited
left behind

You held her rocking
in your rock-like arms
legs braced   sweat running
breath coming in bursting gasps

I could not be there
some things we could not share
—intimacy with your family
you her father with her mother
together again

I waited here alone—
the time seemed long

Then you came home
and told me face aglow
blow by blow
and I listened and shared
a portion of your joy—
how strong she was
how well she'd done
how you had watched
your daughter's baby come

a tiny   black-haired
clear-eyed   pink-skinned
perfectly beautiful
beloved grandson

As he lay dying
(for my friend John Wegrzyn 1977–1980)

1

Will he recognise his memories
without someone to share
them with him?

Trying to follow the trail
and not lose his own
when it crosses another's?

Such a peaceful place alone
to burst the whole world out
a sense of distancing
waiting for the end to reach the end

Beyond the boredom of empty thought
no borders to the here and now
just a body-feeling   everlasting time
totally random   this way   that way

What's it all about?

He has forgotten

The whine of winds
through brain-vast places
becomes a whispered wavelength
in a cowrie shell
waves in the labyrinths
slowed to stillness
to flatness with no dimensions

Without the vision to see
the space in which he lives
unable to pinpoint the now
without perspectives
time has no memory

2

Relativity

As the end comes nearer
time is magnified

Each day seems a month
Each half-year they visit me

Some pay me homage
annually

They've cried so many tears
but they weep for themselves not me

I am their loss   their pain
I feel guilt I cannot explain
knowing they will be bereaved

I suffer and wilt in their presence
but do not complain

I have no wish to be reprieved
If I died suddenly I'd be relieved!

3

Pinned to the bed
by pointed reminders
of a dead past

locked in the final
cage-within-a-cage
the living present
dwindles away in a void
of couldn't-care-less

White-ant-people
tunnel the landscape
inseparable from it
ruled by it
while corrosive forces
obsessed with decay evolve
in the shadow-cracks of walls
acid accusations of blame
and failure waiting to destroy

4

OOBE
(out-of-body experience)

Consciousness rises   a shadow
in the night's dark moment

The shrivelled moon outside
glaring through the panes
beckons almost audibly
beyond my window

I am not alone

Hovering there
staring into my eyes below
sharing a look of agony and dread
my soul's connecting thread
a filament of moonlight
breaking light from shadow
above my head

Surely I dream of escape
—or death?

Though I am deaf
I can hear breathing
Is it my own breath?

Or am I already dead?

5

While they build a fine
mausoleum stone by stone
on a hillside facing the wind

he measures the days at leisure
creating his own time
though without pleasure

In his mind
a day can pass in an instant
a sleep can be a winter's hibernation

Seasons come and go according to his will
spring quickly   summer slow

Sunsets reverse into sunrise

In the illumination of his imagination
dreams are all he has to sustain him now

6

Bleak wind waves
hoon against the granite stone
flow beneath the hollow door
ebbing draughts   eddying dust

Hunched grey shadows
old as the grey day
malingering in the cold room
follow the hush across the empty floor

And they wait at dusk as the day
fades away into dark confusion
Wait in the bereaved quiet
his room a tomb
for a stay of execution

7

I watch
from my mind
a dark corner

(surprising what one can see
from a point of detachment)

They are whispering
lips moving
a silent movie

(I have the advantage)

Behind the barricade
of their pain
their vision is blocked
by pillars of ignorant tears

they kneel and pray
for this husk of grain

praying for me
(preying on me)

Keeping an all-night vigil

Waiting
(impatiently)
for me to die
(again)

8

Hospice

'Tell me—'

'I am in despair!'

'Tell me more—'

'What use is there
spelling it out
word by word
upon my letter-board?

'How much longer will it be
before they wheel *me*
out that door?

'*He* died last night
I envy him

'I watched them sheet him
stealthily

They did not know I saw.'

9

He is drifting   waiting to drown
Sheet quivering icy water
rippling in his double vision

Shivering in a body already cold
he climbs the thin air   gasping

He is drifting   waiting to drown
his hold on life weakening
breath rasping
sinking
down
down
down

10

Too long
I waited
for the day I'd see you
I promised to
but never set the date

Now you've died
and gone away for good
and all the tears I've cried
might make a flood
and show I cared
but not enough

too late

CAMP CREATIVE BINNA BURRA
1977–1985

1

The camp site's freezing
The fire's sneezing bright
sparks on the ground sheet

Diffident along the verge of night they come
drawn by voices   laughter   the smoky heat
the rhythmic beat of music made by men

Rustles slither under rocks   insects
blip and bleep   the forest music background
to this earthy tribe of guitars and flutes

'Hey! Give me E!' Listening intently
'Now A'
The strings are taut aching to play
'I've lost it—sorry!'
"S'OK—don't worry—sock it to 'em!'

Fingers—fine slender wings on hands—fly
along the strings   the notes rise higher
psychedelic subtleties scattering above the fire
The cold air shivers with vibes   grass and trees
tune in to the real existence frequencies
Other guitars pick up the tune   flutes thrill and trill
No force of will can keep the bodies still
or stop them swaying

The swinging stars mark the passage of time
and the fire is dying on the blackened stones
They drift away in twos and threes—the chill
has crept into their knees and stiffening bones

Night closes in around the camp
the fading fire a gradually extinguished lamp
'til one remains

Spellbound I stay to hear him play
his warm mouth kissing the tender flute
while I sit mute

O crying arc
of high-flying song-bird flute
flitting   wheeling   soaring lark
slitting the hollow sky
your fleeting rhythm
calling my heart's beat

In the quiet of my eye
are still black pools
warm with feeling
reflecting your bright joy
Motes of dust the notes
float and drift away
from moonlight into shadow
where remote chords and webs
of tendril silence
grip the forest thoughts
growing in my mind

Quiet becomes silence
for those who sleep
but I hear you   flute
in the listening trees
play on you   fill you with me
and share your joyous melody!

2

Seeing the light

Do You know what I want from You tonight
in this hour before dawn and the coming of light?

I want to ask You what You're all about
I'm no longer afraid—just really spaced out

I'm going to sing to the rising sun
giving birth to the morning—a new day begun

And You have some lessons to share with me
about loving and caring and daring to be!

I'll burn in the sun's existential flames
I no longer fear the fire in my veins

No doubt or confusion consumes my soul
I've got me together! At last I feel whole!

You can teach me the truth about who I am
and I am *me* whether woman or man

I have used You trying to understand
abused You   wasted Your time making plans

and moment by moment You've slipped away
If I don't practise living I won't learn to play!

Your voice in the sunrise is saying to me
'Stop all the conflict! Stop wasting Me!'

I'm learning to play I'm singing Your song
I know You are right I know I've been wrong

O Life! Give me time! Don't go too soon
before I can learn how to play Your tune!

3

The morning after

Grey mist drifts
through the valley of dawn
I try to understand

The morning sun
comes through
and greets the dew

What does it mean
to be a man?

You watched it all
I missed it
Should I try to feel the sun
or be it?

I used to know
Once I saw the sun rise

Will we ever feel it
together?

(Bill Connor)

4

After the silence
when you spoke to me

did you trip on
the track of words?
Did you run breathless
to be near me so
we could say hello?

(Bill Connor)

5

Once you and I
travelling along
the track of life
in the same direction
paused a while
We spoke and touched
before you passed me by

Now
I dream you wait for me
turn and smile

Laughing free I drop my pack
run breathlessly to catch you up . . .

Until I wake to face the fact:
when you waved goodbye
you never looked back

6

From the artist's notebook
Inspired by artist Irene Amos
Camp Creative, Binna Burra 1985

For the artist—
aesthetically oriented
sucking up life like a sponge
noticing everything   impossibly
vulnerable even to words—
sensitivity can become a terrible disease

You put on your surface coat of many colours
and become an actor hiding behind a mask
playing a character full of laughter
never showing the pain of pin-pricking paranoia

You cannot make a mark that is not full of you!
The artist is the medium
a tool of calligraphic energy transposed
and the tool creates the image and the form
the art of life exposed

How to live though—when all art is abstract
the third dimension lost and the better
you cheat the greater the illusion
as complicated as you like to tamper with
yet giving of yourself to it?

You can plan how you hope it will turn out—
dissect your every thought
need a reason for your every move
immobilised in the mire of analysis

Or the emotional approach—exposing feelings
trying to express them coherently
throwing in an ad lib when everything is fighting

The gate is open!
You are released and in a paroxysm of activity
translated as escape run ragged across the canvas
unbalanced between your reason and your passion

O how to fix the mess that's made!
Was time and effort wasted?
No—it is inside you now
the paint of many experiences overlaid
scraped off   washed away   burnt
and disguised in many ways

Have you one hand that's facile and one
so inarticulate it overwhelms you?
Intimidated by your right hand's confidence
does your left hand limply hold the rags and serve?
Left and right brain fight to use the tools
and put the mark down
Paint—and live—with *both* hands!

Do you experience periods of up and down?
Blue Periods enclosed in profound loneliness?
Beggared   grievous   uprooted   pain-filled   alone
emotions expressed as images on the canvas
of your life dominated by one colour
viewed with pity and tenderness by others . . .

. . . the spectators—appreciators—onlookers
Like lovers they are close but not inside your skin
They avoid the danger and trouble being you involves!
They stumble on your path of self-unfoldment
approach your door but do not enter in

Art is for the artist first whose life is on the line
swept up in the maelstrom

Art is the expression of an insatiable lust for life
a mental attitude   a metaphor
for the human mind and spirit

What you think is what you paint
What you feel is how you do it

7

Friendship (for Steve)

Thank you for your open door
Not just a place to stay—
a place to live and be myself
and make peace with my soul

Thank you for your friendship—
warm as sunlight playing across the floor
free as the air blowing in that open door
through which I came and now must leave
to try at home once more

Thank you for sharing your mind and heart with me—
no poem I write can adequately say
what that discovery has meant to me

You are a man I am a woman and we touched
in places no one has touched before
—not just the body soon understood
explored and mapped familiar terrain—

but the spirit—your dreams and motivations
your essential mystery

I paused on the threshold of your life
and caught a glimpse of all that lies within

Thank you for your trust and caring—
for letting me come in

8

Tryst on Heron Island
1977

I have known love
and shared satisfaction
caring without possessing
giving   asking for nothing

You gave me hope
like a new day ahead
I am waiting   without grief
unburdened   ready to fly

You helped me grow to freedom
your time a part of my life
I will leave to fly alone
remembering all you have done

and care again as you cared for me
sheltered under your wing

9

Death—a celebration
(for Peter C) Grafton
1980s

    Imagine late October in a country town
    the Anglican cathedral on a tree-lined
    avenue of jacarandas in full bloom

    There's no-one dressed in black—
    he said he wanted a *gay* funeral!
    Music by Cat Stevens *Morning has broken*
    the closest he let us get to sentimental crap
    No hymns—please—just a few short eulogies
    a prayer or two then the wake
    at his favourite pub in the afternoon

    Wanting—as always—the last say
    he organized the whole shebang
    A *celebration*!

    Of what?
    The disease not one of us
    could bring ourselves to name?
    The fact that gatecrashers outnumber invited guests
    and there's a rockery of wreaths on the cathedral steps?
    That we were at least able to say goodbye
    around his bed at home trying not to cry
    while we watched him die with the aid
    of self-administered morphine?

    We are showered by the perfume of flowers dense
    in the dusty shafts of light pouring down the still air

But it is Rick who is bringing us undone
His once rambunctious pup—presenter of slavering stick
and slimy ball—silent now and still   huddled against the bier
the flowers atop the coffin cascading around his ears
the rays of light through the stained glass creating
a Kirlian aura around the edges of his hair

OF DREAMS AND DISCOVERIES

Of Dreams and Discoveries
by Heather Farmer with Steve Parish
First edition 1979, second edition 1994[1]

For all who dream of discovery . . .

. . . of frogs and fish
with bulging eyes
of childhood dreams
yes
and even feathers
that can fly!

Of lakes and streams
by fading light
of forests green
and deserts brown
of endless skies
and oceans   out
and down

All this
through constant change
with hopes   desires
to re-arrange a life
a dream

a dream of rediscovery!

Steve Parish

---

[1] There are differences in the content of the two editions. In the second edition poems that were in the first edition were left out; new poems were added. The second edition was also accompanied by a CD/DVD titled *Of Dreams and Discoveries*, the music composed by the late Tony O'Connor, who died 23 May 2010 aged 49. Tony was Australia's best-loved composer of relaxation music.

At the risk of confusing the reader, I have 'combined' the two editions and included all the poems from both editions in this compilation. I have also removed the section headings, which were revised/changed in the second edition.

FIRST EDITION
BETWEEN THE LINES

Writing is an expression of experience, uniquely personal. However, the human feelings engendered by experience are universally recognisable, and can be shared.

Several themes pervade this book.

All life is a miracle. Each life is a passage of time.

We can make of life whatever challenges we take up, whatever dreams we make reality. Dreams and hopes are illusions that can become reality, just as despair can become a dream with the passing of time, as hope takes precedence once more.

For some of us, reality is stark tragedy—for the ill and soul-weary a burden too great to bear. Sometimes lives that we long to live, or share, are snatched from us by the quirks of fate, and the answer to the question 'Why me?' comes from another dimension beyond this life's comprehension. To face death with acceptance, whatever the time we have had, whether brief or long, is the greatest challenge of all, made easier if we have not wasted the time we had, made more difficult by regret for not having lived.

For those of us with healthy bodies, an unhappy mind is a shame, a waste of a lifetime, a failure to recognise the miracle of our birth. We have the capacity, when perfect illusions become broken realities, to change and live with joy again—if there is time.

Heather Farmer 1979

Behind the Photographs

In July 1977, world famous jazz musician Don Burrows sat in a cave deep in the rainforest, recreating the emotions he felt in his heart through the music he played on his flute. Fifty metres away, in the seclusion of the rainforest, sat Heather Farmer, pen and paper in hand. Two individuals creatively utilised two seemingly different media with the same ultimate objective: to communicate.

That night Heather recited the result of her experience in the rainforest to the students at Camp Creative, Binna Burra Lodge in Lamington National Park. During the recital, Don quietly improvised on his flute while Tony Groom screened slides of the rainforest.

During those short minutes it took to read the poem I met Heather, and it was because of those minutes that this book evolved. Photography is my medium of self-expression and a means of communication. Speaking freely from the heart on matters personal is something most of us find difficult.

Perhaps, if it was easy, we would never have extended ourselves to create the many art forms through which we humans express ourselves. Each form is an emotional extension of the artist, the writer, the musician.

The natural world can be a source of energy renewal. As a photographer I am fortunate to be able to bring home part of that energy source, in the form of realistic and impressionistic photographs. Captive in my urban fortress, I can view them each time I need that little boost. Further, as one who needs to share experiences, I am able to use photographs as a means of expressing whatever it is I want to communicate.

It is my hope that the photographs in this book can become a source of energy renewal and inspiration for you. Each photograph shares an emotional link with the accompanying poem, but although the notes[2] reveal interpretative reasons for their selection, I trust that you, in your own private world, found excitement in discovering what each one meant to you.

Steve Parish 1979

---

[2] Photographs as well as notes not included here

Instincts unknown

I am the link in the blood-tide
salt flowing through hollow bone
remote and deep in the restless mind
I call the wanderer home

I am my own motivation
the yearning and the obsession
the compulsion without question
mysterious recognition

an impulse
born on the shores of paradise
washed from the infinite stone
repossessed by time   I am the first
an energy source unknown

Creation

Life:
a matter of time
the swelling consciousness
of past and future
a bubble-space of energy
a breathlessly expanding universe

until birth   predestined
dream behind the eyelids
watchful of consciousness
wary of morning
bursts from the dark   fades
in the light
recedes in the yawning wake
sinks into the past
ripples stilled

a memory
no effort can recall

Vulnerability

Strangely twisted
warped
but tender beauty

old   grey-eyed   soft
hollow spaces
hiding secrets for me

In your limbs
strong enough to hold
enfold and hide me
way up inside
your wide high places
safe and carefree

I watched the faces pass
beneath—always hurrying!
Rarely seen by bigger busier
human beings
I stole small moments
from their lives
gave them names and made up
places where they could live inside my games

The indestructible other-world
but they cut you down
for being unsound
fed you to a chip-machine
and widened the road
where you had been

Constant change

Age 5
He drags the bees out of his sticky hair
with a comb of honey from the hive next door

6
Cicadas screech on the flywire
lizards scuttle across the floor
caterpillars munch upon the jasmine
the raucous pond vibrates with frogs galore

10
Now the rock-fiend picks and taps the hills
with deliberate intent   haversack
upon his back   sleeping in a tent

12
Soft! The pelicans are wary of a boy
in his canoe   unsteady camera at the ready
willow-hide disguise paddling in full view

15
Beetles   bugs   butterflies   yabbies
snakes—and birds!
Now he can whistle the sweetest song
a young girl ever heard!

Pipe dreams

Remote-controlled
by a higher mind

a reach-for-the-stars
earth-spun rock
in a void of illusions

Foolish flier
sliding through hydro-space
narcotic-high in the deep
searching for dreams
in a black mist
You think you're awake
but you're really asleep
making light of the dark
as the blind do

A lifestyle unreal
locked in your hermitage
shell-music singing
of seas non-existent

Retreat
and your burning desires diminish
a lonely sage
your dreams unfinished . . .

Searching

The light
a grey beacon

Time a shadow creeping
a tide retreating from the wide wherever

Search   and search for evermore
peer into pools of silent reflection

and find
you don't know
what you're looking for . . .

Independence

I drift away
on the outgoing tide
into the haze with no horizons

able to leave this stage
play the shifting scenes alone
hear my own soliloquy
. . . discover who I am

A moment shared

We passed
soft as a sigh

She was silent music
poetry in action

I smiled
touching her gently with my eyes
as my camera met her gaze in focus

I saw the radiant light
playing with the shadows on her face
For a fraction of a second
the shutter opened wide
and let her look inside
where she burned a vivid impression
of her enigmatic expression
and I captured the charisma of her grace

My eye the camera   the film my retina
the after-image imprinted in my mind
and on this space

Simplicity

We had time

It was not intricate
The melaleucas were not empty

Cool winds blew
across the yielding grasses
Creek beds were not dry

At dawn
in the glow of sunlight
radiant silk
we heard bird songs
passed on from heart to heart
each one alone an empty cry
in unison a symphony
light and songs
caught in a web of music

You caught my eye
as clear pools catch the eye
of morning!

Awareness

A kind of knowing
through premonitions

feeling the answers
to unasked questions

understanding the tensions

wondering wistfully
about the validity
of psychic perceptions

Shyness

I hesitate

withdraw as I reach out
afraid if I grab
you will elude me

Perhaps if I lie
a faker on the grass
blade points
I will attract you

Relax me
touch me with your softness
communicate with smiling eyes
and sensuous grace
alighting lip-first on my face

Afraid   I wait
aching to reciprocate
I might give too much
more than you can take

In love

Like birds on the wing
toe over toe
in joyous flight
cling as we climb
hand over hand
towards the light
tied to the wind

What if we fly
on ethereal highs
through cloud-soft illusions!
Our dreams are welded
to burning desires
flares in the mind's sky
. . . meteorites!

We live for gladness!
Ropes of reality
knot calculation to madness
in a running-line

We will make this climb
with body and mind
to the eyrie of light
the top of a world

. . . this is our time!

Joy
(for Don Burrows)

O crying arc
of high-flying song-bird flute!
Flitting wheeling soaring lark
slitting the hollow sky
your fleeting rhythm
calling my heart's beat

In the quiet of my eye
are still black pools
warm with feeling
reflecting your bright joy!
Motes of dust the notes
float and drift away
from sunlight into shadow
where remote chords and webs
of tendril silence
grip the forest thoughts
growing in my mind

Quiet becomes silence
for those who sleep
but I hear you   flute
in the listening trees
play on you   fill you with me
and share your joyous melody!

Loving

There is life within
exultant   aware
held by the wind
alone in the air

The world has vanished
gone without trace
and the endless sky
is detached in space

A moment of passage
captured in flight
stilled for all time
imprisoned in light!

Laughter!

Mirth unrestrained
escaping from the tongue

Self-communion given voice
shared with a stranger
a friend   a lover
sounds that resound
in the heart of the other
echoing in the mind
long after

A response to the witty
the vulgar   absurd
harmony for the songs of life
sung by the heart

Joy without words

Time

We
never did take time
until it was too late

It passed away
even while we lay on grass
and every plan we made
was an assumption it would wait

Smothering

You grew on me

I was your pillar
your strength
You leaned too heavily

You were not a parasite
but you used me for your own gain
You gave yourself oppressively
and took away my right
to stand alone

I could not grow
You filled my holes
and crushed me with your dream

I crumbled
bone on bone to dust
as you no longer needed me

Misunderstanding

We reach across
the silent space between us
but cannot touch

Nothing is real for us

In spirit we know
the truth remains unspoken
remembering seasons of lies
and promises broken

A burning desire to share
cannot be heard
Afraid to care
we are lost

Without words

Disintegration

We coexist
but cannot relate

I am the wave
that passed you by

You are the rock
that slaps my face

I am the curve
of earth and sky

You the misshapen
uncharted coast

I ebb and flow
you disintegrate

We coexist
but cannot relate

Alienation

Waiting
for the light before the dawn
for that half-forgotten night
to happen again   for rain
and tears to cease
and doubts to leave the mind

Waiting
for the day
when I can be serene
and walk away whether I win
or lose   it's all the same
It is a tedious game
and I no longer choose to play

Waiting
for the sun
and opened eyes
no need to run   no penalties
to pay   You think I play
and wait but you are wrong

Already
I have won

You are too late!

Transition

A lone leaf
clings to a wintry morning
afraid to leave the bough
caught between loneliness
and the fear of falling

Such is the now
a time to choose between two avenues

and the wind is calling

Remembering

The eye within
searching

through the dead-cold
steel-stacked tier-upon-tier
volumes of ancient dreams
edge-torn frail fragments
of memories   read
but unremembered
lodged and referenced
but lost in the dim recesses
of the mind

The ear
ringing imaginary echoes
fading footsteps
receding disintegrations
of whispers
from the past
in the locked and empty
library of time

Running scared

Fear
not imagination
iron cobwebs constricting the chest
relentless pursuit
hissing hatred
hostility manifest

Desperation
a frightened shadow
oblivion a smack in the head
shooting star-dust explosions
with the needle-point question
Asleep?   Or dead?

Relief
is capture   punishment   pain
withdrawal   anger   a shattered brain
obliterated by fear alone
when there is no place
nowhere to run

no home

Fear

Why so disturbed

crawling out of your mind
where darkness shrouds your bones?
What lurks there entombed
whispering in the catacombs?

Beware

Simplify

Lest
caught in a web of consciousness
consumed beyond all reason
you are sucked dry from within
dried up   frail as a snake-shed skin

watched by the mind's eye . . .

Confusion

Lost
uncertain where to go
unsure how to survive
in a burning desert
struggling to breathe
to stay alive
till the scorched heart
stops trying

Life
burnt bare   laid to waste
blackened by the passing
of despair

Who knows what is missing
once it is no longer there?

Loneliness

Desolate
afraid
taunted by time
something I made
carved by my mind

Friendless
solitary
hunting for likeness
searching for kind
in wind-blown emptiness

freedom's bliss
destroyed by loneliness

Restlessness

Time

killed and buried
with guilt
in a secret past

stretches now
long fingers reaching out
treacherous in bones
no longer growing

Time
unfulfilled
climbing blindly
to dizzy heights
caught halfway
unable to complete
begin   create
hanging on
to a dying dream
with painful insight

Despair

Over the edge
they pass
unseeing

yesterday's dreams
disappearing
broken faces
crumbling as they fall

Alone again

No vision of tomorrow
can take their place
I fear her loveliness
resent her almost
knocking at my door
open but not open as her face
I grasp her warmth
but not her trust's intrusion
rasp her with my need
but leave her in confusion

She is today's mirage
in empty space

I must not care too much
Love is an illusion

The death of dreams

I dream of water on a rocky shore
I cannot hear the waves upon the stone
I am an illusion   vapour in the wind
a bleached and hollow shadow
of a life long gone

I dream of seabirds rising as one mind
their scattered thoughts imprinted
in the sand   Atlantis eaten
time will drink the sea   the sun
will shrink   stars fall down holes
into eternity   all that is
no longer will be

I dream of life unlimited
death only is entombed
yet I cannot hear the living wind
in the hushed wing of the bird
I call out to your mind
but my whispers are unheard

I am my shadow
on a never-ending shore
unreal reflections of no influence
when space is time no more

Metamorphosis

Change
not adaptation
is the key to freedom
from the tyranny of the past
the chains of self-imposed conformity
unlocked at last

Transformation
not merely an adjustment
Be what you want to be!
Free to choose direction
Responsible and in control
of now

Accept what is and move ahead
Live! As only you know how!

Facing the challenge

Magic!

Excitement stirs
beyond imagination
surrendering to creativity
and conscious fantasy!

Listen!

Thoughts beyond anxiety and doubt
offer adventure-possibilities
unlimited as mind-potential

The self is not immutable
It is a mystery of body
mind and spirit
Face its challenge!
Be it!
Discover the genius
and the magic in it!

Listening 2

Listen
to the voice of stone
softer than silence
ash of bone
burnt into the sound

Trust the ears
and hear the break of day
the grass-whisper echoes
the thrust of seeds that
grow from their lives' dust
the fire's flame
on the wind's burnt breath
the call of water
seeping below ground
the hiss of rain
in skies as dry as death

All these
like summer sleeping
in the trees have sound
when there are ears to hear
able to listen to truth
without fear

Discovery

Descend vast blue space
into dim cool silence

Enter another world!

Pre-sense out of time
a presence sublime
comprehension
humbling the mind

A macrocosm
Another dimension
A hidden world
in twilight suspension!

Psychic

Here
from another time
another place
in co-existent inner-space
lost futures from antiquity
escaping a catastrophe

We
are their discovery!

Ghosts
from the cosmic memory
drawn by magnetic vortices
through whirlpools to infinity
Surviving a time-warp
they arrive
adrift in our past-life galaxy!

Wonder

Rain
storms the rough bark

Luminous white water
running   trickling
finds its lowest level
every little course not chance
pre-destined hollows
happening because of . . .

Sky-scene: cloud-sculpture
heaps of cumulonimbus
monuments of vapour!
Every shape and nuance
of tumbled grey
conforming to the laws of nature
could not be any other way

Knowledge
revelling in the inexpressible
does not destroy illusion

A fusion of variables
in limitless combinations
the uninhibited beauty
of natural art
awakening wordless feelings
in the scientist-at-heart

Meditation on a raindrop

Wind-water language
of cosmic consciousness

Memory-reflection
of all that has gone by

Living crystal
source of
power and light

Magnetic tear
minute hydro-sphere

In your dimensions
in suspended animation
invisible residents
lie dreaming
transmutations
flying through time
and space
energies captured
dragged through holes
in the sky

Why have you stormed
the earth
your luminous green
glittering brilliance
defying the eye?

Appreciation

In a haze of sun
the lizards creep
from scribbled cracks
on minute feet
tiny monsters from another age
seeking the soporific heat

The gentle hooning wind
whispers sounds of civilisation
to itself   edging
round the crevices
surreptitiously carving
hollow expressions
in the rock shelf

Far below
the river blazes
a silver trail
a glittering scrawl

This vast design of wind and water
is a passing sketch powerfully frail

Time makes small changes
Humans could erase it all

Shame

Shadows
over the edge of night
climb down the twilight
into the canopy of the forest
to hug the living trees

The wind
briefly touching the leaves
can affect the whole
blowing wordless songs
from the fragile emptiness
of dead reeds

A feather
cast from the wing
of a high-flying bird
adrift on oceans of air
sinks down

Seeds
scattered on the earth-bed
lie asleep
beneath the creaking stretch
of branches overhead

A forest
absorbed in growing
awaits the hand of man

Caring

It was caring

six yesterdays unbetrayed
sharing the juice
unpossessive of the fruit
paradise regained

unburdened by guilt or grief
consumed to the heart's core
awareness of satisfaction
reborn to live again

A beautiful thing

a time together   a love
so brief   unforgettable link
in the chain of memory
your gift

and you wear mine
remembering me

Taking care

Look after yourself!
You must!
You cannot give your life
into another's trust

You must take care!
Alone you found yourself
alone you must remain
You will never be free
and in control
while vulnerable to pain

Search the rubble of your security
for vestiges of truth   joys
you knew in your youth
before the bombing began

Go home   trusting yourself
remembering you have changed
It will never be the same
. . . but you can start again!

Friendship

The beginning   like all beginnings
was difficult   a warm wall to lean
against   shelter from the wind
but unyielding to hands
tracing the natural patterns
mysterious map in abstract
of a rugged untraversed land

Exploring takes time   like all discovery
the mind wandering   daunted by shadows
of doubt cast by intercepted light
illuminating the unknown

In the end   simplicity
the silent language of the spirit
breaching the barriers of stone

Serene at last   reaching out
with truth   trust   love
through realms of other-consciousness
I found myself   a friend

Eclipse
(for John Wegrzyn)

Once I wrote
that life was a matter of time
dreaming of birth

Then I discovered you   and you were dying
a malignant silence growing inside your head
We spoke of endings rather than beginnings
of the years you had never lived
of the years you had wasted away
of the years I had wasted trying

Isolation was your greatest dread
and after the operation   lying
in your hospital bed   mutely aware
you stared at my lips   comprehending
the silent words
as I read the poetry of your eyes
mist in dark valleys   colours in rain
the suppliant gestures of your hands
desolate communication

You were reprieved for a time
avoiding the eye of death   but I learnt
gazing over the edge of your life
that the now is all we have left

Ethereal there are no limitations
but life is a matter of time
passing with every breath

Gaia

Alive
beneath benign stars

Veils of light
descend in fading cascades
of inscrutable quiet
broken by laughter of water

Earth smell reaches out

Prising green fingertips
lift the sweet lips of soil
emerging soft-warm
into unexplored dimensions

The wind is tender

No despair is final
growth and repair inevitable

Desiderata

The heart
is set upon a course
to the zenith of ambition
on a flight path
through the ethos within

Dreams re-echo
down mirrors of time
chasing retreating insight
climbing stairways of air
like Icarus to the sun
searching for meaning
the heart   the crux   the core
of burning desires to share
all that life exalts   to care
not for the self alone
but find in another's joy
the joy that is one's own

Follow the will-o-the-wisp
phantom pharos
beacon in eclipse
far above the countenance
of earth
across chasms of confusion
hiatus of despair   flying blind
through cloud illusions
insubstantial as the air
'til burning desires melt
dreams vaporise
everyone
and a life off-course
will come about
guided enlightened

by some magnetic
inner source whose cries
mock and stun
the muffled mirror-image
echoes of reality

For all that is desired
Is where desire first began . . .

A Journey along the edge of The Dreaming
1994

Foreword

The jolt of criticism!

The precious work a synthesis
of experiences while on a journey,
recreated during hours, days and nights,
weeks months and years of rewrites,
re-honed, re-shaped until each poem
seems 'just right'. . .

Now, before peers, the moment
of revelation—the *exposé*—
the exposure to vulnerability,
purple passages an expression
of inner being . . .

Imagine being dismissed!
Well, no, not quite dismissed.
Condemned.
No, not condemned.
Confronted. Challenged. Analysed.

'The ideology is dented. The narrator is,'
(it will no doubt be pointed out)
'proselytising, propagandising, preaching,
passing judgement from a superior height
as she journeys through her ideological landscape—
in other words, getting her political rocks off.'

'The narrator must experience conflict
where her righteousness and feelings of guilt
come up against other equally obvious
Indigenous realities—violence, child abuse,
drug misuse, alcoholism, incarceration . . .'

This is true.
The narrator does not—and may never—have answers
but hopefully through the eyes and minds of her characters
readers' minds might also change through time

Red, white and true-blue

The tourist coach is full of whites
A few are coloured by extremes
Their comfort stops are pubs—coarse
seams of alcohol extrude through stony faces
Their necks are red as desert dust
Bodies oozing sweat reek of ancient lust

Colonial frontier values mist the windows of their eyes
They speak crude ignorance and arrogance—clones
built on lies knowing nothing more than their own histories
twisted blue-veined fingers pointing their own bones

Riddled with patriarchy they are blind
the culture of convict ancestry
predisposing them to cancer of the mind

Taree
(wild fig tree)

On the edge of town the homes
of fenced in Aborigines
housing commission enclaves
fringed with trees adjacent to
their forests—now the State's

Coolongolook:

On either side future telegraph poles
reach high startling masts in the dark
of canopy and undergrowth
Ahead the black snake highway
clogged with cars writhes
through *Bulahdelah Gap*

Paddocks brittle dry
where massacres took place are empty now
cleared of their people and their trees
Bulldozed mangled limbs and amputated trunks
lie distorted   funeral pyres waiting to be burnt

Ash fogs the air
a smokescreen like the history she learnt

Australia has a black history 1

'They do not court a life of labour . . .
that of our shepherds and hut-keepers
our splitters and bullock-drivers . . .
of unmeaning toil . . . they would
by no means consent to exchange
their free unhoused condition
for the monotonous drudgery
of such a dreary existence.'

Select Committee on the Aborigines
New South Wales Legislative Council
V and P, 1845, p. 17

Karuah

A beautiful country

Seen through ancient eyes
the past becomes the present
The ancestors hold on
their bones in the earth
As if knowing descendants will return
spirit children wait to be reborn

The wattle blooms again
Beside the road   up to its eyes in grass
a wallaby   alive   is living dangerously

Unaware   the strangers
in their air-conditioned capsules
cruise   like lethal bullets
through *The Dreaming*

Ahead salt-water oyster beds
Hotels   motels   cemeteries
respite for the living and the dead

Stop!   Revive!   Survive!

Report chemical spills immediately!
Emergency phones 3 km and 9 km respectively
Protect our waters from pollution!

Life
becomes more dangerous

Warnings
the only solution

Mobil   Fast food   Hamburgers

Signs warn of secret police   the dangers of speed

Crumpled wrecks of cars   slices of life and death
are splattered on screaming billboards
mourning modern massacres

Roadworks smash the earth   bulldozers crush rocks
steamrollers flatten   mountains are carted away
in trucks   dust obscures meaning

A few inadequate trees prop up the sky
which leans dangerously   like glass
Listless dusty withered cows
graze the sparse dry yellow grass

The barbs on wire fences cannot contain the past

Liverpool Plains

A warning buzz   a leaking valve
'We're losing air—a minor hitch!'
Inside the coach the pax slump back
slack in the stale atmosphere
The smokers stir   then grasp
the opportunity to join the crew
They stand there   cigarettes cupped in hands
exchanging nicotine for air
'til everyone and everything is fixed

The river is a trickle
The vast plain undulates and stretches
unsettled by a weary emptiness
Whirling drought-dry winds swirl
around the cardboard cattle   cut outs
standing motionless in dirt-bare feedlots
their shoulders hunched   eyes
half-closed to the dust and glare

The blue-ice sky is streaked with white
All the trees have the same lean
The wind   relentless   bows them down
The grass is longer but not greener
on the road side of the fence
Each stalk gleams   wind-blasted
to a sheen in the late-day light

The grass leans like the trees
whose long shadows
stand over the dying landscape
with threatening gestures
Did Wiradjuri Wirrayaraay burn here?
Create this space?
Lush pasture for kangaroo and emu?
Was this the place?

1838 on Henry Dangar's Myall Creek Station
on the Liverpool Plains a brutal massacre
Twenty-eight black men women and children dead

'See that smashed wooden horse-float up ahead?
The horse inside musta got excited—
kicked the back to splinters 'n fell out
I ran right over the bugger's head!
They didn't hafta waste a bullet on 'im!' the driver said.

Australia has a black history 2

The Reverend Lancelot Edward Threlkeld, married to the daughter of the colony's surgeon, supported by Archdeacon (later Bishop) William Broughton, calculated that in the region of his mission and westward into the Liverpool Plains five hundred Aboriginal people were massacred in an eighteen-month period.

'. . . a war of extirpation . . . in which the ripping open of the bellies of the blacks alive; the roasting of them in that state in triangularly made log fires, made for the very purpose; the dashing of infants upon the stones; the confining of a party in a hut . . . letting them out singly through a doorway to be butchered as they endeavoured to escape . . . with many other atrocious acts of cruelty which are but the sports of monsters boasting of superior intellect . . .'

Annual Report, 1837
Rev. Lancelot Edward Threlkeld

    Do not close
    the book though
    it is horrifying
    to read!

    Look at the facts
    the acts
    of a 'civilised' nation

    Denial
    is the name of the game
    we have been taught to play
    since the beginning of our education

Coolah   Dunedoo   Dubbo

Sheep are dots of ochre on sand
cattle blobs of umber
on the red-black ground
reminiscent of Aboriginal art

Trenches slash the landscape
farmers at war with the forces
of erosion   even the teeming
rabbits seem despondent

Ploughs gouge dark symmetries
across the plain   a soft green
struggles through the cicatrices
responding to one false shower of rain

Morse code shadows flicker on the windscreen
mirroring the sun between the trees
apart from creatures dead on the roadside edge
the stricken land seems empty   *terra nullius*

Cattle in the stench of treeless feedlots
are protected from an accidental death
Trapped behind electrified wire
their time to expire is on a calendar instead

West   into the sun   clouds have been hung
along the horizon ominous and full of promise
She overhears a passenger complain:
'A four-year drought surely guarantees
our first night sleeping out will be free of rain!'

The Western Plains

Minus three at dawn
no warning
of the day to come

The military museum
an ancient battleground
strewn with dead bodies
—skeletal remains of artillery
tanks   trucks   jeeps
the sun's long rays
searching for signs of life

Pink-fleeced sheep lurch thirstily
across the dam's cracked heat
Irrigated paddocks—glimmering green
—are slashed by blades of hopeful wheat
Farmhouses shimmer in the rising temperature
—bricks of earth-warm local clay
in the kiln of another fiery day

Blanched leaves and strips of bark fall to the ground
nipped by pink-and-grey galahs in the ghost-white
branches of senescent trees stripped of their blossoms—
red drops of blood on pale green fingertips

The harsh uncompromising scene
is softened by a pastel sky but the marshes
where great egrets nest are almost dry

West Wyalong Centenary 1894–1994

Following the muddy Murrumbidgee
the highway—once a bullock track
winding between makeshift tin huts
on the goldfields—brings them to
their comfort stop and morning tea

Some seek the pub but she
discovers a country café—
raspberry muffins clotted cream
and cappuccino coffee
Fellow travellers from Moree
with scones and jam and pots of tea
join her for company

The couple talk of cotton crops and sprays
bank managers bankrupt farmers
and the drought generally:
'Their daily diet is bread and rice—'
'These folks have used up all their funds
their debts are astronomical—'
'They're buying food on borrowed money
too proud to ask for charity—'
'Even if or when it rains I doubt
they'll get on their feet again—'
'It will come too late to help them out!'

The muffins are dry—there's not enough cream
She'd like to complain and ask for more but refrains

Husband and wife speak together again:
'Pity about the Aboriginal problem!'
'No reason why the two races shouldn't get along.'

In silent contemplation she drinks her coffee

More a Gubba problem don't you think?
We inadvertently attribute blame just by the name!
Saying they're the problem seems quite wrong—
so much depends upon the point of view.

The couple sip their tea   lick the cream
from their fingers   flick the flies from their eyes
They return to rain when they speak again—
the weather is a safer topic

A rubbishy tale 1

Beer cans   spirit bottles   broken glass
silver bladders of Coolabah casks
soft-drink bottles   cardboard cartons
car bodies   car parts   petrol drums
plastic bags stuffed with unwashed tins
and fly-blown barbequed remains
overflow stinking roadside bins
ghastly eyesores   ugly metaphors
ironical slaps-in-the-face
for the creators of enormous waste
confronted with their own poor taste

DISPOSE OF RUBBISH THOUGHTFULLY

Meaning out of sight   out of mind
in someone else's backyard not mine
Near the riverbank on the edge of town
in the Aborigines' centuries old domain
By all means transport radio-active waste
out of the cities   ten thousand drums
and a quarter of a million years
of contamination are not *my* problem—
as long as it's not in *my* state
or anywhere near *my* place!

Rubbish is thrown from trucks and cars
all along *our* highways and *we* hate it!
'How ugly!'—*we* say—'How can *they* desecrate
the landscape in this way?'

A rubbishy tale 2

Imagine an Aboriginal perspective
What might the elders say?

How to dispose of *gubba* rubbish
—thoughtfully or otherwise—
is not within their Law
They've never had to deal with 'rubbish'
in their lives before

Now they use our products and packaging
without adequate means for their disposal
Fleets of compactor trucks and teams
in every community would cost a lot of money
Gubbamen grants would be needed to get them
underway and keep them going every day
They'd need trained mechanics for maintenance
money for petrol or diesel fuel and oil
money for the drivers' and collectors' pay
money for wheelie-bins—for landfill and recycling
though there's no recycling plants
—or plans—out this way

They didn't have to think about such things
until the *Gubbamen* appropriated ancestral land
for rubbish dumps and nuclear testing
rocket ranges and defence training
sheep and cattle stations—and let loose
rabbits and foxes   camels and horses
goats and pigs   donkeys and buffalo
rats and cane toads   cats and dogs
laid oil pipelines   gouged open-cut mines
built toxic drains and railway lines
introduced diseases like STDs and AIDS
traded alcohol tobacco and other drugs
too numerous to name . . .

The custodians of the land didn't have to worry
about such things before the *Gubbamen* came
Now they too drink alcohol
while their kids sniff petrol
to also numb their brains

A rubbishy tale 3

While some of us
perceive our own detritus
as evidence of decadence and desecration
and recognise it is a problem
with international dimensions
there may be others who consider
the garbage piled up against the fences
to be the artifacts of civilization—
the tins and bottles and casks along the highways
affirmations of western influence and affluence
—aesthetic creations not disgusting aberrations

Bush Tucker Dreaming

How conditioned she is!
Nails painted and filed
teeth flossed Macleans smile
soaped and powdered
denuded of oil
underarms deodorised
no sweat escaping to soil
washed and ironed designer clothes
perfume hanging in the air
hat on shampooed conditioned hair
sunscreened skin with Aerogard
thrown in to deter those pesky flies
hovering around her eyes

Nevertheless—she feels so shy!
Struck dumb   afraid to say
the wrong thing
wanting to know everything!

She watches the Aboriginal
woman painting a boomerang
Honey ants and witchety grubs
—long lines of them each side
and in the middle acacia roots
in brown and white and red
'Bush tucker Dreaming' she said

Her hair is matted her tattered skirt
splattered with paint
She sits in the dust a twig for a brush
which she dips into lids then dots it
on the surface of the wood painting
with concentration and precision

The stranger uncomprehending
a deep ancient secret is unfolding

Kings Canyon

Seeds scratch seeds   a seeds-in-a-gourd rattle
Hanging between the hakea's harsh dry leaves
are small green fruits on bead-string stems
Mistletoe dangles from long-leafed eucalypt limbs
River red gums stretch and rise from the creek bed
white in the bright light   leaf-tips effervescent
with flowers and insect wings
Small brown wrens with cocksure tails
scuff through leaf mulch raising dust
Gold nests of spinifex
nurse the rays of afternoon sun

Between the glowing coals of rocks
smoky black spinifex has died back
in the furnace heat   a red rock lizard—
the bug-eyed frilled-neck rough-skinned kind
—rests on the cliff's long edge
leaning sleepily against the sky

Ants skirt the cooler shadows line-dancing
to the buzz of crickets   the hum of flies

This path—a riverbed winding around chunks
of rough-hewn sandstone carved by flash floods
and gully winds—was used by *Ananga Maru*
but intruders won't see an emu or kangaroo here
let alone *Anangu Maru* passing through
Visitors' voices—chattering gossiping
laughing questioning joking competing
—disquiet the atmosphere

Imagine another time   a similar cacophony
as *Ananga Maru* children approach
the campfire's sizzling catch laughing
playing leaping from stone to stone
bare toes clinging   imprinting the red sand
There's a different pattern now—Reebok
Nike   Adidas—exotic sets of wedges
zigzags logos dots and spots

Snaps

Under the slow gaze
of late afternoon
mist and drizzle
puddle together
on bleak corners

Too cold to sit
with bottles empty
playing cards wet
old men shelter
in doorways
huddled together
spitting and talking
ignoring tourists
walking by
who pause
for a quick snap
of their plight
in the poor light

Beneath
paperbark trees
freeze-dried on park benches
rimy with the salt of sweat
drug pedlars deep in debt
pencil-thin sharp as needles
not so old are dying young
hawking

PEACEFUL EARTH
1996 AND 2021

I wrote the lyrics for *Peaceful Earth* in 1996 while living in Grafton. The album was recorded at Bruce Vickery's Recording Studios, the lyrics sung by my niece Carolyn Ferrie, the music composed by Bruce Vickery and Len E Johnson and the album published as DVDs.

Recently, the album was uploaded online and can be accessed on forty sites including iTunes, Apple Music, Amazon Music, YouTube Music, Spotify etc.

Search for: Ferrie Farmer Johnson Vickery Peaceful Earth

Glass of heaven

Is there no way back
to what has been?
Innocence   an Earth pristine
clear as the glass of heaven?

Flaming ruby   jewel of fire
Rub' al Khali   cinder fireflies
ash on the glass of heaven

Snows drifting   ice-fields growing
wild wind's breath coldly blows
mist on the glass of heaven

Air rare   mountains high
glaciers bare reflect the sky
blue on the glass of heaven

With sun and moon
Earth a fragile place
in air cocooned in darkest space
A secret tear   blue-green sphere
a planet with air for atmosphere
breathes on the glass
clings to the glass of heaven

Gaia living Earth   air   fire   water
breathing life   giving birth
to her first daughter
mirrored in the glass of heaven

Is there no way back to what has been?
Innocence   an Earth pristine?
Clear is the glass   air is the glass
clear as the glass of heaven

Fire

Cherished beliefs bring sweet relief to human minds
Nations sing blind hymns of praise for their causes

With God on both sides of Holy/Just wars
Who in God's name can win? Can win?

(Chorus)
Never again was the refrain
(Repeat)

Waters recoil rainbows in oil animal destruction maximal
Oil wells on fire dire for *Gaia Amun-Ra* day star blood red fire

(Chorus)
Never again was the refrain
(Repeat)

Weeping they pray give us this day our daily bread
return our dead   children of nations   no destination
mass migrations   obliteration

(Chorus)
Is war what life is for? Is war what life is for?
Is war what life is for? Is war what life is for?

Never again   was the refrain   never again
never again   no more . . .

Listening

(Chorus)
Listening   listening to you
(Repeat)

There's still time still time to change
still time to change our relationship

There's still time still time to save
still time to save our long partnership

It will be a long climb just the same
we know we are to blame   we play a dangerous game
be in loving harmony   are we insane?

(Chorus)
Listening   listening to you
(Repeat)

For too long too long we've used used and abused you
had our own way   losing you is a price we can't pay

You were fine your life divine you were fine
until we came to stay didn't listen too much to say
We gave you gave you a hard time gave you a hard time
and misery we are shamed by our inhumanity

(Chorus)
Listening   listening to you
(Repeat)

Let's make peace a lasting peace
Looking at Earth's ravaged face
hard to believe what we've done
see what we've done to this place

There's still time still time to heal still time
to stop the violation still time for reconciliation

Let's make peace for our families
Let's have peace in our communities

Listening   listening to you
We're listening to you listening to you now

Peaceful Earth

Senseless violence what was the gain?
A planet destroyed consumed by flame
Offence defence the end the same
The cost immense nothing won but pain
while foes return from whence they came
no recompense for all the songs they sang

Sane minds hindsight can see the light
It's not too late to heal the pain to try again
Earth air fire rain   Earth our mother
and *Amun-Ra*   need one another
cannot have one without the other

(Chorus)
Violence it makes no sense
Earth needs our reverence
(Repeat)

Who do we think we are?
Invaders from a distant star
exploring time and space?
Malignant aliens?
Now our disgrace is colonised Earth
Defaced effaced for all she's worth
To be replaced when there's a dearth

(Chorus)
Violence it makes no sense
Earth needs our reverence
(Repeat)

A peaceful Earth among the stars
green blue and white
Amun-Ra raining sunlight

(Chorus)
Violence it makes no sense
Earth needs our reverence
Violence it makes no sense
oh no   Earth needs our reverence
Violence it makes no sense   no more

Reverence

Peaceful Earth among the stars raining sunlight
Planet of water   blue   green   white   peaceful Earth
Winds are blowing rivers flowing water running clean
Grasses sowing flowers opening forests growing green

Earth is mothering   Earth is mothering from her womb
Mother Earth is recovering   is recovering from her wounds

Nothing on Earth to show they came
Nothing on Earth sojourn erased wasted by *The Flame*
Earth smells are reaching out   prising green fingertips
lifting the soil's sweet lips emerging soft and warm
into the air devoutly

Earth is recovering   is recovering from her wounds
Earth is mothering   mothering from her womb
Earth is mother   will recover   ahhh

Peaceful Earth among the stars night and day

Earth is recovering   is recovering from her wounds
Earth is mother   will recover   oohhh
Earth is mothering   Earth is mothering from her womb
Earth is mother   will recover   ahhh

THE 1990s

Variations on a theme

Cherished beliefs
drip down the plughole
into the sewers of small minds

With God on both sides
of Holy/Just wars
who—in God's name—
can win?

Rainbows in oil
are filth to the wind

Give us this day
to reap what we sow
to know what we spoil

The refugees
make their getaway
crowd onto spaceship Earth
spin three million Ks each day
a lifetime journey
in search of a haven

a long way one-way
trip to Heaven

Middle East

This assault
is a mistake of war—
a horrifying misjudgement!
Nostrodamus got it right
for sure

We have to blame the leaders—
not say some young
button-presser
got it wrong!

It's coming up now!
The scene looks like daylight
—technically demanding—
too much contrast
between the black of night
and the searing atomic white

The destruction of a whole city—
old people   mothers   children in their beds
all dead—like ants in a mound turned with a spade
immolated with a blow torch and sprayed

I couldn't show this footage over there—
the censors had moved in
I didn't want it confiscated
or me end up in prison some place
so I left it in the bottom of my suitcase
and when we fled I smuggled it through
security undetected and brought it home

They wouldn't have wanted *this*
on their evening news—the population
would have become unnerved
The dead don't talk—

but reporters and cameras do
People on the move put a strain
on services blocking the roads
begging for water and food
holding up the military passing through

As for our various enemies—they weren't
to be allowed to know the damage done
The code was: admit nothing
Poo-poo their puny efforts to bring us down

The censors struck the zeros off civilian casualties
and reduced each 1000 to 1
They said if we pin-pointed targets on the news
the next attack would be on our own heads
So we agreed to leave and crossed the border
and focused on the living—the refugees—instead

I'm telling you confidentially Doc
—to explain my nerves

I showed it to my boys
but they didn't find it interesting—
without enthusiastic commentary
the soundtrack's just a lot of noise

The TV's blaring news—between the ads—about
the war but no one's listening . . . so repetitive
it doesn't have an impact any more
My kids prefer playing video games
Violence   rape   starvation
mass destruction have become a bore

A script for Tranx please Doc should do the trick
and maybe something else to help me sleep?

I'll keep this for the home library
and show the grandkids one day—if I have any.

State Ward

Fear is the dark hallway
cobwebs constricting his chest
toilet too high and hissing
hostility manifest

Woman smells sweet—
sick-sweet reek of alcohol
and lust on loveless streets
his manic mother—laughing now
with heroin on the bed
smoking playing stroking
the top of his unwashed head
while he stands on tip-toe
beside her pillow
He knows no other
only that time will bring a lull
and the question—is she asleep
or dead?

Fear is when she wakes
—tears punishment and pain—
depressive anger beating pulses
in her shattered brain
But time brings pleasure
with the fear of being alone
Alone is good—she might bring food
if she comes back again

She does come back again
She lets the sunlight in—
and yet another stranger
—flinging back the door
swaying down the corridor
crying: 'I do the best I can!'

Too late he senses danger
'He's a neglected child!'
Tries to withdraw his terrified hand
'It's time!'
Dragging unwilling feet
'I don't want to go!' into the street
Away from her away from home
the only home he's ever known

Friendship

We were lovers of life   plunging the depths
climbing the heights   trekking through forests
and snowfields together   rebellious canoes
running down the white water tumbling
the pebbles of umber and amber drowning
our voices with silver-sound clamour

We shared our happiness   kept our freedom
shattered illusions   built on reality
listened with humour and equanimity
to each other's dreams aspirations discoveries
Exploring the wild we found each other
growing together with trust and laughter

Friendship permanent as life itself—
but life can be fleeting and transitory!
Fate arranged that we should not meet
on your last frontier—a city street
Time alone should have taken your life—
to be crushed by a truck like an avalanche
seemed a tragic irony

Beneath the sea

Sea anemone
anemone
See the enemy
shark swirling silently
swiftly surreptitious
shadow sleek

Anemones
coloured flowers of the sea
in clefts and cracks
on hillsides facing
the tidal winds
sipped by butterfly fish
floating between the weeds

And I like an eagle
soar on the current
or lurk in the kelp
blowing bubbles of compressed air
a stranger a danger
another shark a scavenger
sea enemy
anemone
anemone

Predator

The damn cat's there again
sphynx-like lynx-like
the colour of sand
and sharp shadow
blending in
with the foliage
and flowers
of the honeysuckle

The bird-feeder keeps
tilting and swaying
under the impact
of landing lorikeets

the ginger cat
lies in wait
directly underneath

Raging Thunder

The raft tilts for an instant
poised on the edge of the glass
water stilled by a trick of the light
before it plunges into
the whirling boiling vortex
sucking hungrily with gaping mouth

The tiny craft is engulfed
swallowed then spat out
its six occupants consumed
dragged below rolling over and over
round and round possibly drowned

The raft spins this way and that way
desperately seeking its occupants
One by one plastic helmets— with humans
attached—pop up like colourful bubbles

Buoyed by life vests they strike
with flailing arms the face of the water
pushing and pummelling towards the raft

'They cling to the sides of the grey
floating island frantically signalling one another
voiceless in the raging thunder

POEMS FOR THE NEW MILLENNIUM
2000–2021

Snake

Run over
guts split
splattered on the highway

Life
a hiss
of electricity
short-circuited

a modern rainbow

The Bullrocks

Monumental sea lions jostle
for space on the ledges
scarred carcasses
pitted and ravaged
savaged hulks ulcerated
the burst bubbles' petrified edges
oozing dark blood staining red
the bruised blue shale
and slate-grey skin

Carved from gaping caverns
they sprawl below the worn-out
worn-down mother-of-a-cliff
a rubbled hillside now
dense with banksia and bitou
where tense and tiny birds
hide from predatory crows

High above the violence of the sea
the bullrocks lie impervious
to the sights and sounds of history:
thrashing storms and wailing winds
trashing the sails of tall ships
come to grief foundering on the reef
sailors floundering drowning sinking
down tossed to and fro in the tidal surge

Far away along the bay the surf
a thundering refrain roars
like an incessant train emerging
from the underground pulling up again
and again on the shore of the twenty-first century

The bullrocks sprawl along the ledge

peering over the edge of time
ageing imperceptibly

Beneath the waves in hollows and caves
the skeletons of ships and dead men lie half-buried
Overhead a murder of crows
black-garbed crones cawing a dirge
Crucifix shadows fall from their wings casting a pall
chilling the sand-filled skulls and salt-burnt bones

Untethered

The spacecraft recedes
a tiny light in the darkness
barely distinguishable among the stars

Gravitational waves warping space
undulate her severed lifeline
with slow grace

Her short and tiny life
as she has known and lived it
has come to an end

The helmeted spacesuit
protecting her body
will become her shroud

She will float in limbo
never to reach the shores
of the universe forever dead . . .

That's the trouble with this job—
gloomy thoughts run wild
out of control inside your head
reflecting the blackness beyond

Your inner space becomes crowded with
hallucinations dreams deceptive delusions
fixations phobias compulsions obsessions

You can't switch your brain OFF
unlike the robots and computers—
in sleep mode they at least get a rest
from themselves . . .

Hotel Trivago

In the rabbit warren city constrained
in her small den her tiny cell millionth
in a hive swarming with life she is programmed
to wait behind plate glass—door locked and chained
in switched on sunlight counterfeit warmth and
recirculated air month after month
lulled by the hum of electricity
and pap regurgitated on TV

Sustained by bottled water and red wines
she stares unblinking at the plasma screen
munching salted cashews roasted in oil
Observing starving skeletons she dines
on chocolate-coated health bars wrapped in foil
inured to violence and war scenes
mothers crying their children at death's door
Trauma repeated soon becomes a bore

unable to hold the likes of her in thrall
Tectonic plates shift and lift the Earth's crust
Seismic reverberations tear the ground
Tsunami waves pour over city walls
Thousands—people and animals—are drowned
mushed beneath the flotsam and jetsam thrust
The waters ebb—the landscape and slaughter
reminiscent of old Hiroshima

Shrines mosques pagodas temples cathedrals
homes schools hospitals markets shops all crushed
Nuclear reactors explode and melt down
shrouding the country in a toxic pall
Residents evacuate town by town
Geiger counters click in the deathly hush
measuring the soaring radiation
Bored with this rerun of devastation

she abandons the nation to its fate
idly surfing the channels with the remote
Pausing at an erupting volcano
she watches villagers fleeing too late
the pyroclastic surge and lava flow
engulfing them and their huts—ash clouds coat
the planet flights are cancelled planes grounded
travellers stranded officials hounded

She falls asleep in a wine-induced daze
Cocooned by dark-tinted double-glazed glass
Outside and down above and below ground
machines travel a psychedelic maze
emitting a cacophony of sound
sirens wailing horns blasting as they pass
bright enucleate discs of red and white
flooding the city's bloodstream with their light

An alarm at dawn wakes her from the dead
beeping her from bed into piped water
Sweetened and whitened artificially
strong percolated coffee clears her head
She consumes Special K with UHT
dresses applies lipstick and mascara
Armed with the latest in technology
and plastic electronic ID key

she falls into the void down ninety floors
As she exits underground her eyes glaze
Mesmerised she merges into the throng
queueing to board the long travelators
One among millions she is moved along
finally surfacing into a haze
of exhaust fumes and a deluge of noise
with all the other robot humanoids

Gun Culture

Whatever its size weight calibre or type
a gun is guaranteed to maim or kill
One human being can easily wipe
out dozens of unarmed victims at will
Admittedly somewhat haphazardly
but practice develops accuracy
Even a toddler can fire a small gun
shooting the baby or grandma with one

Guns are essential not just optional
Hoarding a multitude of guns makes sense
It's useful to maintain an arsenal
whether for defence or to cause offence
Whatever the arbitrary reason
regardless of time or place or season
you have to be ready to make the call
not be caught unarmed your back to the wall

Guns are useful but they're impersonal
—interceding twixt firing and demise
Knives on the other hand are personal
—it's YOU who stab cut slice incise excise
scalp or flay—it's YOU filleting the fish
carving the meat or quartering the quiche
paring your toenails or dicing the cheese
or carving initials in the trunks of trees

Mobile launchers fired at the heavens
shatter airliners passengers and bags
Kalashnikovs and AK47s
are carried proudly often wrapped in flags
Be it a medley of missiles or mini rockets
or bullets in revolvers in pockets
or deadly flick-knives secreted in sleeves
or displayed on belts in holsters or sheaths . . .

a gun is useful—a knife personal
They say armaments are for survival
There'll never be disarmament or peace
while we human beings are armed to the teeth
For what it's worth while living on the Earth
every human should carry both from birth

Trumped
2015–2020

The Don outshone upstaged put in the shade
every other presidential candidate
His exaggerations bare-faced lies and hate
eclipsed surpassed outdid out-laid out-weighed
all his opponents—GOP and Democrat
Prevarications were his stock-in-trade
his online lies an encyclopaedia
of 'alternative facts'—Trumpedia—
his late-night Twitter tweets a crazy tirade
against the so-called 'fake news' media

Some saw a psychopath—others 'a ghoul'
Either way *something* was wrong with Trump's brain
'Climate change fake news!' his constant refrain
Aggression greed and selfishness the rule
'The world will bow to US power again!'
He dropped 'the mother of all bombs' on cruel
ISIS terrorists in Afghanistan
and fired missiles against Shiite Syrian
Alawite President Assad ('a fool')
and Shayrat airbase 'because,' he said, 'I can!'

Though Sunni Saudis oppress their women
Trump sold them a billion dollars of arm-
aments so they could inflict maximum harm
on Shiite Houthi 'terrorists' in Yemen
wedging Sunni and Shiite Islam
baiting the Saudi's Shiite neighbour Iran
Trump tweeted a running commentary
as the potential catalyst for world war three
unfurled on TV and this crazy man
'Made America great again!' by decree

What if Dictator Trump should win again
and QAnon conspiracies prevail?
there'll be reduced ability to vote by mail
unfettered police power will remain
'Black Lives Matter' will be of no avail—
and Republican militias will gain
kudos as the president's private army—
'Stand back and stand by' as Trump said calmly
America will *never* be great again
Until the states are *United* by democracy

Danger signs

Warning!
Danger!
Toxic Materials!
Carbon dioxide!
Caustic soda!
Chemical Waste Storage!
Chlorine gas!
Corrosive liquids!
Cyanide!
Flammable gas!
Hazardous atmosphere!
Hazardous Chemical Storage Area!
Hazardous waste!
Health hazard!
High Voltage!
Hydrochloric Acid!
Nuclear weapons!
Radiation contamination!
Polluted water—do not drink or swim!
Do not enter!
Pesticide Storage!
Poisonous toxic chemicals!!
Report chemical spills immediately!
Protect water from pollution!
Beware!
Robot Moves Without Warning!
Keep Away!
Look Out!
Keep Off!
Keep Out!

Caution—
Dangerous cancerous malodorous treacherous *Homo sapiens*!

Another perspective

Peering through telephoto lens
across the face of the rainforest pond
into the dim cool silence beyond
I enter the ants' micro-world
where luxuriant forests
of lichens and mosses
unfurl on a mountainous log

Within that log are citadels
where highly evolved societies dwell
whose denizens are citizens
antipodal to democracy
fully employed as
miners and tunnellers
housekeepers and weavers
hunters and gatherers
herders and cultivators
loggers and chippers
builders and carpenters
architects of edifices
passages and bridges
paranoid loyalists
protectionist royalists
programmed demolishers
with armies of soldiers
omnivorous colonists
as ruthless and exploitative
as we—their mortal enemy

Their middle-earth kivas are microscopic extensions
of a total environment in need of protection
While I watch the ants—a long-lens surveillance
who—with what—watches me?

Christmas haikus

Children and parents
sing carols by candlelight
Christ's birth glorified

In the dead of night
sleighbells herald the coming
Santa by moonlight

Ancient floorboards creak
whisp'ring parents bearing gifts
enter on tiptoe

Children sneak a peek
pretending to be asleep
no one knows they know

A long time ago
three wise old men on camels
came with gifts for Christ

Let us dream and pray
we can live in harmony
just for this one day

Each of us a link
in a golden chain of peace
stretching 'round the world

Resurrection

Imagine Earth
recovered from her wounds

Forests again cover mountains
New species graze on the plains

Cities long-drowned by the rising seas
Freeways reduced to rubble beneath the dunes
Roads and railways overgrown
All signs of human endeavour obscured
A brief sojourn erased

Beneath the grass and stones
lie empires and nations
whole populations imprisoned
buried in the chalk of their bones

None has risen
Ashes to ashes dust to dust reclaimed

Earth
lives again
lush with the spring rain

The search for meaning

Professor George Smoot
author of *Wrinkles in Time*
sat somewhere and reflected
on where we came from

peering back through time
to the very first second
the birth of the universe
creation's moment

Since that first second
13.8 billion years
ago (give or take a few)
God must have aged too!

Was *this* universe
also born from another?
(Maybe God has a mother!)
A co-incidence?

Or an accident?
Or created by design?
Life should have been and almost
is impossible

Had another sperm
racing through his mother's womb
won the race it would have meant
no Idi Amin

no Pol Pot   Hitler
or the frightful Ghengis Khan
Likewise slight variations
in God's position

might have prevented
our very own universe
from being squeezed through a black hole
Can you imagine?

Does it matter there
are other kinds of matter?
Does it matter how time and
space actually formed?
Does it matter what
was there before God was born?
13.8 billion years
is just a minute

a minute fraction
of time for our universe
Space and time are relative
Albert Einstein said

Relatively speaking
my life is just a flicker!
An instant of momentous
significance to me!

It's time to make the
best of it—to take the most
from it! As for the future—
let's just wait and see!

www.ingramcontent.com/pod-product-compliance
Lightning Source LLC
Chambersburg PA
CBHW071957290426
44109CB00018B/2046